KIDNAPPING
RONNIE

PATRICK KING & TUDOR GATES

First published in Great Britain in 2006 by
Allison & Busby Limited
13 Charlotte Mews
London W1T 4EJ
www.allisonandbusby.com

A catalogue record for this book is available from
the British Library.

10 9 8 7 6 5 4 3 2 1

ISBN 0 7490 8297 6 (Hardback)

ISBN 0 7490 8160 0 (Trade paperback)

Printed and bound in Wales by
Creative Print and Design, Ebbw Vale

PATRICK KING has worked as an investigative journalist for national newspapers and as a producer for current affairs programmes for television including the top rated *The Cook Report*. Currently he is a writer, producer and director of historical documentary films for international broadcasters.

TUDOR GATES is the author of five novels and three non-fiction works. He is also a West End playwright, a producer and director, and has many feature screenplay credits, including successful cult movies such as *Barbarella* and *The Vampire Lovers*.

ACKNOWLEDGEMENTS

The authors would like to thank the team at Allison & Busby – Susie Dunlop, Lara Dafert, Chiara Priorelli, Louise Watson and Mia Kilroy – for their enthusiastic support throughout, as we would Michael Zeffertt for his patient correcting of seemingly endless drafts. Also to all the organisations and individuals who helped with our research. Finally to family, friends and associates – too numerous to list – for their assistance and constant encouragement.

PREFACE

When I was asked to write this book I was at first reluctant. My involvement in the international security world had been a long time ago. I had since built a reputation as a successful documentary filmmaker and as a rule kept my adventurous past to myself. Within months of the book offer however, I was approached to co-produce a documentary titled *Kidnap Ronnie Biggs* by those who knew that I, as a young man, had been personally involved in the affair. Why the sudden interest in Ronnie Biggs?

Although only a minor player in the Great Train Robbery, Biggs has been hitting the headlines since his arrest and conviction in 1963 for his part in the £3 million heist (worth £60 million today). Since escaping from prison in 1965, Biggs' exploits had made news time and time again as he evaded capture by Scotland Yard.

When, in 1974, he was given sanctuary by Brazil's military dictatorship Biggs turned himself into a celebrity. With the help of the tabloid press, he sold himself as the 'loveable rogue', the first real celebrity criminal, even dedicating his autobiography to his 'fans'.

Biggs' public presence was undoubtedly a constant irritant to the British Establishment and something had to be done about it. Perhaps that is why he was snatched from Brazil in 1981, by a team of ex-servicemen, and taken to a Caribbean island, friendly to Britain, to await extradition. It was the ultimate press story and soon a frenzy ensued as journalists speculated wildly on who was involved in such a caper. The tabloids, caring little for the truth, were only desperate for the next day's headlines.

The Biggs affair wasn't the most dangerous or even the most interesting mission I have been involved in but it certainly was the most publicised. Tired of reading speculative and inaccurate stories about the operation, I was persuaded by close friends in the media to break my silence of twenty-five years and finally to give my account of those bizarre events that led to the kidnapping of Ronnie in 1981.

I suggested to the publishers that we have two authors: Tudor Gates would write an objective overview of the mission and Ronnie's early life, while I wrote a personal tale. I had, fortunately, kept the operational log of the mission as well as photographs, 8mm film and all the receipts.

During our initial research we encountered a problem over the availability of reliable written material about Ronnie Biggs. Apart from a book and some excellent articles by Colin Mackenzie, the *Daily Express* journalist involved with Biggs in 1974, the accuracy of the rest was doubtful for our project. It would have been too easy to regurgitate all the old stories about Biggs, his escapes from the law and finally his abduction from Rio in 1981. Ronnie, of course, has had two major books published about his life and mentions the kidnapping in one of them. John Miller, leader of the kidnap team, also wrote an account of the abduction in a book. Their books however, contain a number of errors, which have unfortunately been perpetuated over the years. We decided it was best not to use this material, except for the odd date reference or other items of undisputed fact.

For the book's main theme, kidnapping Ronnie, we decided to rely heavily on personal accounts of the many people involved. Recollections obtained through interviews, either by us or sources we knew.

An important source of information came from my former colleague Sylvia Jones. A respected television producer and journalist, Sylvia had secured exclusive access to Scotland Yard files on the Great Train Robbery and Ronald Biggs. This was particularly useful in putting together Biggs' early life and showed how his wife, Charmian, had played a much bigger part in handling Ronnie's share of the robbery money than had previously been admitted in interviews. The documents, many previously classified, are now available at the Public Records Office in London.

But, to give this book authenticity, it was vital for us to secure the full cooperation of Tony Marriage and Fred Prime, two other important members of the snatch team who had never before talked publicly. Their agreement to be interviewed by the authors has given the book an exclusive insight into their part of the story.

Their first-hand accounts of the sea voyage while guarding Ronnie is fascinating, as were Tony's recollections of our time in Rio. Fred's contribution was essential for us to understand what happened in Rio in 1979 when John Miller and he met Biggs for the first time.

Unfortunately we were unable to trace Mark Algate, the fifth member of the team, or Thorfinn Maciver, skipper of the *Nowcani II*, the yacht hired to take Biggs from Brazil to Barbados. This book therefore only contains statements they both made openly to me in conversation or to the press when the story first broke.

We talked to numerous people from Brazil, Barbados and Britain who were involved at the time including journalists, policemen, diplomats, former criminals and to Biggs' legal team in 1981. Fortunately our task was made easier by the passage of time, twenty-five years after the event these people, some unable to comment at the time, now talked openly. Retired Brazilian Police Chief Carlos Garcia gave a particularly fascinating account of Scotland Yard's attempt to seize Biggs in 1974, and how on one occasion he ordered Superintendent Jack Slipper to be handcuffed.

Whenever possible we cross-checked information, but often had to rely on the memories of the people involved. Therefore the authors cannot be held responsible for any hazy recollection of details twenty-five years after the event. In addition, my personal account is written as I interpreted events at the time. Although the members of the team were and have remained friends, I have described all the tensions, frustrations and arguments that inevitably arise during such an enterprise.

The final chapters in Part Five trace the whereabouts of all the key players. I've also mentioned a few other high profile 'kidnaps'. The very word 'kidnap' is naturally an emotive one. Hostage taking usually falls into two categories: a criminal kidnap, where a ransom is involved, or a political kidnap, where a political concession is demanded. Kidnapping Ronnie was neither. When a government kidnaps a fugitive from a safe-haven, it is conveniently referred to as a 'judicial abduction'. My hope is that this chapter will provide more of an insight into the background to our mission.

Finally, to appreciate the events described in this book one has to understand the political climate that existed in Britain and the West during the late 1970s and early 1980s. It must also be remembered, especially by the younger generation, that the operation to snatch Biggs was planned before the current technological revolution had taken place – there were no emails, no PCs, no mobile phones, not even faxes.

A few years ago a former American Green Beret Colonel told me 'Time doesn't change the truth, people do by altering it'. Rather a lot of fiction seems to have crept into previous accounts of this extraordinary caper, mainly, I suspect, due to lack of information. I believe this book now sets the record straight.

Patrick King
London, February 2006

Brazil, fifth largest country in the world

PROLOGUE

When the mark finally arrived at Sugar Loaf, they were ready. But he was fortunate: that lucky star of Ronnie Biggs was still shining down. The taxi he was in arrived at the entrance behind a coach that was disgorging a load of tourists and, as the cab came to a halt, another coach drew up behind and quickly started to empty its load.

The team looked on in disbelief as Biggs was immediately engulfed in a jostling throng, trying to make their way in. Their chances of a snatch at that precise moment were exactly zero! Ronnie could just be seen walking up the stairs and entering the restaurant.

'Lucky bastard!' said someone.

John Miller took charge at once. This was what he was good at, thinking fast, going into action.

'Look,' he said, 'we can't let him get away. This is our last chance. It's as simple as that.'

PART ONE

What happened before…

CRIME AND PUNISHMENT

It was Thursday, August 8th 1963. The travelling Post Office was making a routine, overnight journey from Glasgow to London. On board was the usual team of sorters – the process was then a manual one – working through mailbags, pigeon holing postcards to Aunt Mary, final demands from hire purchase companies, never to be repeated offers of the chance to win a fortune.

Deposited in the first carriages after the locomotive there really was a fortune, about three million pounds in Bank of England notes, something like a sixty million pounds at today's value, which were being returned to various clearing banks in London. What is more, they were used and untraceable – a bank robber's dream.

When they approached Sears Crossing in Buckinghamshire, some thirty miles from London, and the signal showed red, the driver suspected nothing. Jack Mills braked the train to a halt and, seeing that the signal beyond was green, suspected a fault and sent his fireman, David Whitby, to investigate.

The first thing Whitby discovered was that the phone link had been cut. The next thing he knew, he was surrounded by a mob of menacing, hooded thugs. He needed no second warning to obey their instructions to the letter, and was not hurt. Jack Mills was less fortunate. When the gang swarmed on to the footplate he suffered a severe head injury from which he would never fully recover.

The Great Train Robbery, as it was instantly and affectionately dubbed, was conducted like a military operation; the thieves even had mock army vehicles and walkie-talkies.

The postal sorters attempted a brief defence but capitulated under armed threat. All the remaining coaches were uncoupled and the gang prepared to move the engine and its precious cargo to a more convenient site, to unload it: every last detail was meticulously planned.

The one hitch of the night occurred when an old train driver, nearing retirement, whom they had brought with them to move the engine, found himself in some difficulties with a modern diesel. He insisted he only needed time to get the pressure up, but the impatient gang could not wait. Instead, they forced the shocked and badly injured Jack Mills to move it for them.

Most of the crooks were either efficient and silent or scared and unable to talk. But one of them was on a high, with adrenalin flowing. He chatted cheerfully with the captured railmen, even scrounged a cigarette from one of them.

He ignored the glares of the other members of the gang, some of whom had been against his inclusion. They were pros, heavyweights, and he was a small-time villain, recruited only because he had once served time with their leader, and had claimed he was able to provide an essential ingredient, the person to drive the train. In their eyes, the old man had turned out to be a bumbling, senile fool, the one useless component of a brilliantly executed crime, one which was to capture the public imagination probably more than any other before or since.

Yet this amiable incompetent member of the gang is the one whose name is most likely to spring to mind when you ask anyone about the Great Train Robbery.

He was Ronnie Biggs.

* * *

After counting their winnings and sharing out the proceeds, tasks which took them some days owing to the magnitude of their haul, the robbers began to disperse, but not before a group of 'cleaners' from among the gang had washed down every surface which could possibly bear their fingerprints. In this way, when Leatherslade Farm, the gang's unoccupied hiding place, was eventually discovered by the police, there would be no proof of any kind that any member had been involved. They would be suspected individually, of course, because of their previous criminal activities, with the exception of the old train driver who had no record, and indeed would never be found. As a second line of insurance, once they were all clear, a 'dustman' had been booked to come in and set fire to the farmhouse.

Various members of the gang had made reconnaissance trips to establish whether there were any road blocks set up by the police, at the same time buying motor vehicles in order to make good their escape. Biggs left Leatherslade with his old colleague Bruce Reynolds, who had master-minded the adventure. They departed bold as brass in a flashy open-top Austin Healey roadster.

En route, they discussed what they would do with the money. Ronnie was planning to dribble his share of the proceeds into the building and carpentry business he had started up at the behest of his young wife, in order to go straight. He had sworn to her many times that this was all he ever wanted to do but, somehow, all such plans never worked out.

Bruce Reynolds delivered Ronnie to the door and then left him with his delighted but greatly apprehensive wife. Charmian knew her husband well enough by now, and of his past association with Bruce. It soon became pretty clear to her just what her husband's absence on a 'tree-felling' expedition had really been.

Ronnie reassured her that they had come out of this absolutely clean and that nothing could lead the police to them other than suspicion, certainly not proof. The amount of money overcame her scruples and Charmian assisted her husband in counting the notes, £150,000*, even burning off any which they believed might in any way be identifiable. After which they had a night out, celebrating modestly.

The next day the money was counted into portions of around £60,000, which were picked up by, or delivered in suitcases to, 'minders' who would, for an agreed fee, look after the money until it was required, in effect operate as personal bankers.

It was not long however before the police did come calling on Ronald Biggs because, though he was not told this at the time of his arrest, his prints had been found at the farmhouse, on a Monopoly set and a sauce bottle. In spite of the gang's meticulous preparations, the 'cleaners' had overlooked just these two small items, handled without concern by an over-confident petty criminal who had been operating out of his depth. It was not a great deal of evidence but it was enough to put Ronald Arthur Biggs and most of his fellow-conspirators into the dock.

Biggs' first trial, in company with the other defendants, began on January 20th 1964. Although still considered a minor figure, a petty criminal, he was the first to make the headlines, a capacity for which he was never to lose. An inexperienced police inspector, giving evidence, fell into the trap of quoting Biggs directly. When asked whether he knew any of the men wanted for the train robbery, the detective stated that Biggs had replied: 'I know Reynolds, I met him when we were doing time together.'

So that the members of the jury should remain impartial, the law is that none of them should know of a defendant's previous record. After a quick discussion with his counsel, Biggs on advice pleaded for, indeed insisted on, a re-trial. Back in gaol, on remand, he was able to follow with great interest the trials of his fellow-conspirators. Only one, John Daly, was to be acquitted because, crucially, the jury accepted his plea

---

* worth £3,000,000 today

that the Monopoly board, on which his fingerprints were found, could have been carried to the farmhouse subsequently.

Since his own prints had also been found on the board, for a while Biggs held high hopes that he too might get away with it. However, the same identifying marks were also discovered on a bottle of sauce and, when he came up for re-trial on April 8th, he stood before a jury which was considerably less open-minded about such matters.

The main trial ended on March 28th when, with the exception of John Wheater, a solicitor who had been involved in the conveyancing of Leatherslade Farm, the remaining defendants were found guilty.

At the re-trial, Biggs called a number of witnesses, including his wife, to support the intricate alibi he had concocted. The prospects of an acquittal, so long as the Biggs company could keep up the pantomime, were reasonably good but, while Biggs played his part skilfully, one of his key witnesses took fright and did not turn up to commit the necessary perjury. Thereafter, in Biggs' view, the judge was prejudiced and the foreman of the jury hostile. The previous occupant of Leatherslade was in court to swear that the sauce bottle had not been there when he left and this evidence, together with the suspicious circumstances of the missing witness, was enough for him to be convicted. All that remained was the subsequent court appearance at which all the gang would receive sentence.

Only Bruce Reynolds and Buster Edwards were not present. Roger Cordrey was the first to be called: he had pleaded guilty to the conspiracy charge only. His plea had been accepted and, while he still expected a longish prison sentence, he was stunned by the twenty years awarded. The next one hoping for some kind of leniency was Billy Boal, who in fact had not been present at the robbery at all. He was still found guilty along with the rest on both counts, of conspiracy and of robbery with violence. He was by far the oldest of the bunch and the judge must have known that he was giving Boal a life sentence when he gave him twenty-four years. Billy Boal, who was quite innocent of the main charge, was indeed to die in prison. It was a day for harsh sentences and exemplary punishment.

The others knew what to expect. Charlie Wilson, who was next up, got thirty years on the robbery with violence charge. Biggs got the same along with five other members of the gang. The sentences were fierce, even vicious, greater in term than those meted out to murderers. Even those employed on the periphery of the operation were treated in the same harsh way.

The message was clear: those who tamper with Her Majesty's Royal Mail do so at a terrible risk. The sheer audacity of the enterprise had made fools of the State's institutions and the State hit back with a vengeance.

Most people must have thought that they had heard the last of Ronnie Biggs and the other great train robbers for a very long time, but they were soon to be proved quite wrong.

THE FIRST GREAT ESCAPE

On the same day his appeal was turned down, Ronald Biggs was transferred from Brixton to Wandsworth where he was categorised as a security risk, a 'special watch' prisoner. There was no parole system in place at that time as there is today, and the train robbers faced the serious prospect of serving out their thirty years in prison. Not surprisingly, the thoughts of Ronnie Biggs turned immediately to escaping, a course of action he even threatened in a letter to his Brixton Member of Parliament, Marcus Lipton, complaining about the excessively long sentences imposed on the gang.

The first one to make a break for it was Charlie Wilson who, perhaps with premeditation, had opted to stay at Winson Green Prison in Birmingham rather than appeal and be transferred to another gaol. In an efficient and brilliantly planned escape, he was somehow spirited over the wall and into a waiting car by three unknown accomplices. The date was August 12th 1966, and it was to be three and a half years before he was arrested again – this time by the Royal Canadian Mounted Police!

While the exploit re-ignited public interest in the robbers and was welcomed by them as a gesture of defiance, a finger up to the authorities, they were also well aware there would be a price to pay for this enthusiasm. As they expected, every security measure was tightened and then re-tightened.

Warders were put on guard night and day outside Biggs'

cell, with visual checks being made every fifteen minutes or so. In addition, he was moved from cell to cell without warning, often in the middle of the night. Wherever he went in the prison during the day, he was closely accompanied. Biggs even felt constrained, though possibly with tongue in cheek, to complain to the governor that such treatment was affecting his health. The governor was not moved by Biggs' display of his trembling hands: he had had experience of this prisoner on previous occasions.

Needless to say, all the extra security precautions served only to encourage Biggs into perfecting some kind of plan. For this he would need the help of others and he took every opportunity, during the compulsory exercise periods in the yard, to recruit assistance. Everyone approached was keen. There existed, curiously, a kind of mass resentment towards the authorities for having been so unfair in their treatment of the train robbers, not for jailing them but for condemning them to such impossible lengths of imprisonment. There was also, of course, the kudos that would be attached to anyone in the criminal world for having helped a great train robber to escape: they would have their own brief period of fame, costly though it might be.

To overcome the stringent restrictions placed on him, Biggs devised a brilliantly simple plan. Crucial to the attempt would be the part played by Paul Seabourne, a fellow convict, who was due very shortly to be released, thus enabling him to undertake the necessary arrangements outside while Biggs still had to figure out how he could be on the right spot at the exact time when his rescuers made their appearance.

The principal problem was the scaling of the 25 foot high wall that surrounded the prison yard and they came up with an ingenious solution. A high-roofed furniture pantechnicon would be acquired by Paul and, at an appropriate time, parked alongside and close to the prison wall. Even the pantechnicon's roof, however, reached no higher than some five feet below the level of the parapet. Biggs' expertise as a carpenter allowed him to design a five foot high rostrum which could be levered up from inside the van to a height where it effectively formed a bridge with the top of the wall.

Paul Seabourne and his friends, suitably masked, would then let rope ladders down into the yard for Biggs and anyone he chose to accompany him on the break-out, so long as they could evade the watching screws. When they reached the top of the wall, they would cross the makeshift bridge and leap down through the roof on to a pile of mattresses, by which time the sole remaining task would be to get the hell out of the area before the proverbial hit the fan.

Timing was of the essence. There were two exercise breaks and prisoners never knew whether they were on the first or second: selection was entirely arbitrary. In order to synchronise their movements, the escapees had to be in the yard at exactly two p.m., during the second period. This necessitated a great deal of play-acting, feigning a variety of medical conditions, in order to miss the first one.

Even so, exercise in the yard only took place during clement weather and, on the first day of the planned outbreak, strictly according to sod's law, it rained. Fortunately, Paul Seabourne was well aware of Wandsworth's rules and so promptly aborted the operation for that day.

The next day, however, July 8th 1965, the sun shone brightly. Happily, the ruses that had served to make them miss the first exercise period on the previous day worked again. Two fellow cons had been lined up to tackle the warders who were always supervising Biggs, allowing him to sprint to the wall. For some weeks he had spent time getting himself to a peak of fitness. His companion would be an old friend from earlier prison days, Eric Flower, recently sentenced to serve twelve years for armed robbery.

In the event, the operation went like clockwork. Soon after they had started their exercise, a heavy vehicle was heard lumbering to a halt on the other side of the wall. Within minutes, a stocking-faced head appeared at the parapet and two rope ladders were snaking down. Whistles blew frantically as the warders came running, only to be met and wrestled to the ground half-way by the two heavyweight accomplices.

In the courtyard there was total chaos, allowing two other prisoners to follow Biggs and Flower up the ladders. They did not have a clue as to what was waiting on the other side but time and tide wait for no man. They too leaped down into the furniture van, preventing Paul Seabourne from setting light to its contents, as was planned.

Two other friends were waiting in the escape car nearby and it was a scene of complete farce as Biggs and Flower jumped down from the van and piled into the car, only to be followed by their unexpected companions who also wanted a lift to freedom. All of them were jumbled together in the rear seats of the car, desperately trying to remove their prison uniforms and yet stay out of sight in the impossibly cramped conditions.

There was no outward sign of an immediate chase but they still went ahead with the pre-arranged switch to a second car, allowing the two opportunists to keep the first one and make good their own escape. In a backwater of Dulwich, they parked the 'clean' second car and then strolled casually to the nearby safe house. The plan had worked brilliantly so far, from start to finish, but the main game had yet to begin.

Ronald Arthur Biggs had pulled off his first great escape and, overnight, had become the most famous of the train robbers. Suddenly he was a household name.

Everyone likes to see authority ridiculed. The man in the street's reaction was more one of amusement rather than outrage, such public anger as there was being directed against the supposed custodians rather than the escapees.

The theme was echoed by the newspapers, where pages were devoted to the incident, complete with diagrams, timetables and artists' impressions of the cleverly devised plan. Biggs' name made every headline and the front pages all bore his photograph, either the stern prison mug shot or a more natural grinning, cheeky image. He had taken his first step towards becoming some kind of national working-class hero.

The publicity delighted him but he was only too aware that it could also prove problematic. These two facets would dictate the pattern of his life over the next forty years, when his exploits would make him number one on Britain's most wanted list. But it was not only Wandsworth's governor and the police who wanted to see Biggs back behind bars.

There were other forces at work too.

THE SECOND GREAT ESCAPE

The British government was embarrassed. True, the principal scapegoats for the Biggs fiasco were the governor of Wandsworth and his staff, but the ultimate responsibility rested with the Home Office. The police and the courts had done their jobs and put the lawbreakers behind bars, those they had caught, anyway. Bruce Reynolds and Buster Edwards were still at large as well as the other members of the gang whose identities were not, and never would be, known to them. Two had been professional enough to wear gloves throughout the whole operation and the other was the old man, the would-be train driver.

The public wanted to know what the point was, anyway, of locking them all up – no matter for how long – if the gaols could not hold them? First, Wilson had escaped from Winson Green and now Biggs had made fools of everyone with his audacious escapade.

In doing so, he had become famous, the first topic of conversation in public bars and at private dinner parties, at every level of the social strata. There was not a corner of the land where Biggs was not discussed. To the public at large, he was something of a hero. The way they saw it, he and his mates had stolen money only from banks, which was a welcome change from having the banks steal money from them. They were unaware of the insignificant part he had played in the actual crime: the impertinence of his escape had promoted him to being, in the public eye, one of the masterminds.

The more strait-laced considered that the whole operation, from start to finish, had demonstrated only the total incompetence of the authorities: the government, Royal Mail, the police and the staff at Wandsworth, especially the hapless governor.

They wanted to know what the government was going to do about it, but unfortunately the government hadn't a clue as to what could be done. They could not interfere with the operations of the police who were currently occupied in trying to round up the rest of the gang, those convicted and un-convicted. And it was hardly a job for the armed forces. Was it a matter that should be referred to the intelligence agencies?

For the time being, it was decided that the police should be allowed to bear sole responsibility for the capture and recapture of the criminals at large. As in all matters involving national security, however, the Biggs affair did not go unnoticed in the more shadowy corridors of Whitehall.

The principal object of this nationwide interest, one Ronald Arthur Biggs, was meanwhile holed up together with Eric Flower, his fellow escapee, in the upper flat of a semi-detached house in respectable Dulwich.

Biggs was comfortable enough there – he had a knack of making himself comfortable anywhere – but Flower was unhappy with the arrangement. His argument was that the police were bound to turn over Paul Seabourne, a known close associate, which would inevitably lead them to Paul's own associates. Eric preferred the anonymity of the East End, followed perhaps by a countryside hide-out. He slipped out to make a few phone-calls and, the next day, two heavies arrived to whisk them to a house in Bermondsey.

Eric Flower's surmise had been correct. Within days the Flying Squad had descended on Paul, who was subsequently arrested for assisting in the escape, convicted, and sent back to prison for four and a half years. Meanwhile, the two escapees had transferred lodgings again, this time to Camberwell, where more friends of Eric came up with a comprehensive travel package, designed specifically for them, which included a boat trip to France, accommodation at a Paris clinic where a plastic surgeon would alter their features, new passports and airline tickets to any requested destination. This was all for a price, of course, the equivalent at today's rates of more than a million pounds, a large proportion of Biggs' share of the proceeds from the robbery!

Biggs was still hot news however, and it was felt wise to delay the journey for a few weeks, to allow things to cool off. They kept on the move, at first going to a house in South London where their host was an Irishman and unbelievably a private detective by profession.

Plans were finalised for their trip abroad. This involved being disguised as merchant seamen for the cross-channel journey. As they strolled out of the dock gates in Antwerp, a car miraculously stopped to offer them a lift to Paris. There they were given new passports – Biggs was henceforth to be Ronald King – and a minder was waiting to take care of them in their new apartment.

After a few days to settle in, they were taken to see their plastic surgeon who agreed to operate on them at the weekend. Although Biggs had been looking forward to the event, uncomfortably aware that his picture had figured prominently in the newspapers both at home and abroad, he was taken aback to see Eric Flower, who had been done first, emerge from the theatre with his face totally encased in bloodied bandages and with two straws sticking out from his nostrils to allow him to breathe.

It was too late for second thoughts. Biggs was wheeled in to receive the extremely painful treatment and the two men were then given beds at the clinic where they spent a week of agonising convalescence.

Eventually, they returned to the apartment where plans had been made for their final chosen destination – Australia. Eric, who had recovered more quickly than Ronnie, was told he would be first to go and, within days, was telephoning to report on the delights of Sydney.

Eric's operation had been largely a matter of reducing an over-large nose while Ronnie got the complete works. He did not much care for the results, which had smoothed his face and eyes to give him an almost Oriental look, and it was still blotched and swollen. Informed that it would be a week or two before he could proceed on the next leg of his escape, he told his minders that he wanted a last celebration with his wife and family before leaving for his new life abroad.

Before long, closely watched – though not by the police – Charmian was on a ferry crossing the Channel, using a passport with her single name, together with the children. There was some discomfiture on the kids' part at Daddy's new look but they soon adjusted to his new appearance and got used to it.

They booked in at a hotel and had a wonderful few days, spending freely. They went to shows and ate in expensive restaurants. The kids were taken to parks and museums and the zoo. It was a Christmas to remember but, on December 29th, the message came that it was time to move on. Biggs received yet another passport, as part of the package, this time in the name of Terence Furminger.

The New Year of 1966 was imminent and the family's joint resolution was for a happy and prosperous new life down under. Australia, though it did not know it, was about to welcome a new citizen, one Terence Furminger, alias Ronald Arthur Biggs.

Arriving in Sydney, Mr Furminger made his way to the familiar sounding King's Cross area where he saw in the New Year alone, toasting his success with cans of ice-cold lager from the bar in his hotel room.

Eric Flower – or Bob Burley, as he now was – had checked out of his hotel so Mr Furminger left a message, sure that he would call in. He took a day or two looking round Sydney, trying out the numerous bars and making friends with his affable hosts. He visited the racecourse, hiring a taxi for the whole day to see the sights as well. Stan, the cab driver, was a close mate by the end of the day, even providing an address where mail could be delivered. Biggs needed that for Charmian to continue sending him money.

Eric at last showed up and there was a joyful reunion for the two escapees from Wandsworth. Eric had settled in and was already working as a petrol-pump attendant under his assumed name. He was revelling in the Australian way of life, which he recommended with enthusiasm to his pal Ronnie.

It had begun to look as though Sydney was the place where they could both put down roots. That was until Stan arrived one day, anxious because the Post Office had checked the pages of a *Country Life* magazine sent to Mr Furminger and found some UK banknotes had been interleaved. Ronnie talked it over with Eric and they both decided it was time to up sticks. Biggs bought a car which Eric, a useful mechanic, stripped down to make sure it was right for the journey and then, driving through the night, they travelled south to Adelaide.

To be on the safe side, Biggs changed his surname back to King, one of several aliases he adopted in Australia. This was not a good idea because he was quite forgetful and would often give the wrong name when he had been introduced as someone else. His quick wit and ready charm, however, always extricated him from such delicate situations.

Eric remained Bob Burley and got another job at a service station. Ronnie moved into a guesthouse and found a job in a joinery factory. He made many friends and was a ready helper at the guesthouse, eventually proposing a partnership with the proprietor. He had ensconced himself comfortably enough but he still pined for his wife and kids.

The travel agents had not been inactive at home. Once they were satisfied Charmian was not under police surveillance, they organised a flight out to Darwin for her, travelling as Mrs Furminger. Ronnie was delighted. Eric's wife and child had already arrived and were soon settled in. The two families could get together and start their new lives in Australia.

Charmian had brought with her a tranche of the remaining proceeds of the robbery money. With all the expense involved in keeping people quiet, it was reducing fast. Ronnie took a job as a carpenter again, earning good wages with plenty of overtime.

Charmian became pregnant, and after Farley's birth in April 1967, life was looking really good for the Biggs family, now the Kings. As ever, it was not to last and when an anonymous letter arrived, informing them that the police knew of their presence in Australia the family moved to Melbourne.

Life stayed on an even keel for them right up to 1969, when Bruce Reynolds was finally caught in Torquay: he too had been smuggled abroad but could not resist the lure of home. As ringleader of the operation, he got twenty-five years.

In March of 1969, Frances Reynolds, Bruce's wife, told the story of their years on the run in *Woman's Weekly*, which was quickly copied around the world, including a splash in the Australian *Woman's Weekly*, with plentiful illustrations, not excluding one full-face of Ronald Arthur Biggs.

To make matters worse, a Reuters correspondent had found out that the Australian police suspected Biggs was living in Melbourne with his family, under assumed names, and published this information as a news item which was rapidly picked up by the press countrywide.

Ever the optimist, Ronnie was all for lying low until the storm blew over but Charmian had a presentiment: she told him that he had to leave and that she and the kids would somehow manage to get by. Ronnie was forty by this time and she could not bear the thought of his being locked up until he was an old man.

She drove him to a motel near the airport where he checked

in under yet another name. They made arrangements to meet that night in a Chinese restaurant – if the coast was clear. During the day Ronnie called to say he needed his razor and some other toiletries, all forgotten in the rush to get away, and she promised to bring them with her.

There were no obvious signs that the house was being watched and at the appointed time she left the children in the care of Nicky, the eldest, and set off to drive to town. She had got little further than the end of the street when she was suddenly, terrifyingly, blocked by a whole posse of police cars, sirens blaring, that came from all angles and surrounded her car. Some dozen police officers waving guns ordered her to step out, then searched the interior, presumably looking for Ronnie.

When they did not find him, Charmian was accompanied back to the house, in case he was hiding out, but the bird had flown. If the Australian police had simply followed Charmian instead of stopping her, Ronnie Biggs' adventure would have been halted in its tracks. Instead of which, it was to start up all over again.

When she failed to appear for their rendezvous, it was pretty clear to Ronnie what had happened, as was subsequently confirmed on radio and television. Charmian had been arrested and put into gaol. The children had been allowed to stay with neighbours at first but were then taken into care.

All this drove Charmian frantic. She deeply loved her children yet could do nothing for them but weep in a flea-infested prison cell, her sole companion a filthy drunk, stinking of urine and faeces.

Ronnie had done a flit in double quick time. He called on a friend – somehow he was always able to call on friends – for help, and was boarded overnight, then drove high up into Melbourne's Donderong Mountains where his mate had a holiday shack. For a few days, with plenty of food, magazines and a radio, he was able to hole up in comfort, until disturbed by news on the radio that the Biggs manhunt had shifted to the Donderong Mountains. He realised it was time to go.

He knew by now that it was no longer a question of shifting from city to city. He was known positively to be in Australia and he could never go back to Charmian and the kids: it was time to get out altogether, to another country.

That was no easy solution. The police had mounted road-blocks and were watching airports, seaports and railway stations. Even if he had been able to negotiate these obstacles there was still the question of wherewithal. The money, probably from the robbery, Charmian had brought over was long gone and he was virtually penniless. Always with Biggs, however, at the darkest hour the clouds parted and Lady Luck shone down on him. He read in the papers that Charmian had sold her story to the Kerry Packer group of newspapers, which must have brought in some much needed cash. It would be difficult getting a message through to her but not impossible.

What he needed now was the assistance of another friend, preferably someone who also knew Charmian and would be able to get in touch with her. A feature of Ronnie Biggs' life on-the-run was always the willingness of friends – often little more than acquaintances – to help him out, even when they knew his identity and therefore what consequences there might be for them.

In this case, the friend chosen was Michael Haynes, a selection not without risks since he was a known associate. However, luck was with him once again – he discovered the police had not so far contacted Haynes. It was too dangerous to take the chance to stay with him but Mike knew a young English couple living nearby who generously, though nervously, agreed to put up the wanted man, who certainly had reason to be thankful for the kindness of strangers.

It took a long time for the dust to settle, although the focus of the manhunt did shift for a while. Ron Flower, alias Bob Burley, was arrested in Sydney on September 27th. Biggs still had to lie low, relying on his instinct to tell him when it would be time to make a move. In the meantime he could plan, and he plotted his expedition abroad as carefully as any tourist, eventually selecting Brazil, home to so many German war criminals and therefore plainly having a relaxed attitude with regard to asylum seekers. Besides, it had wonderful scenery – he was much taken with the Sugar Loaf – seemingly endless golden beaches peopled with thousands of stunning golden-brown beauties in the flimsiest of swimwear. It had been a long time since Biggs had enjoyed the comforts of the matrimonial bed.

Christmas arrived and the Haynes' went off to spend it with Charmian, partly to assure her Ronnie was alive and well, partly to pick up the first payment of her fee for the newspaper story, to facilitate his move abroad.

The limits of friendship are often quite extraordinary and Michael Haynes was even willing to surrender his own passport for Ronnie's use. The photograph was cleverly removed and replaced and the new Michael Haynes was ready to book his passage and board the SS *Elloris*, a Greek ship bound for Panama in February.

ROAD TO RIO

Having first disembarked at Panama, he travelled by air via Caracas, at the same time purchasing a ticket for Montevideo just as a blind. When he left the plane at Rio, he stood there alone, early in the morning, blinking at the sun, with the Sugar Loaf as a backdrop and two hundred dollars in his pocket – a man whose previous forays had only been while on the run from the police, whose only language was his native Cockney with a bit of 'Strine' thrown in when necessary.

As always, he had made a friend while travelling, an elderly American gentleman, bound for Argentina but stopping off at Rio to see some friends. While Bill, his new-found friend, checked in at the Luxor, Ronnie was obliged to find a flea-pit of a hotel in the town, well away from the golden beaches. He soon discovered that the brochure descriptions applied only to Copacabana and Ipanema. Where he was staying, the bay was too polluted for swimming and a noxious odour blew inland from the waters that were black rather than blue.

He took a look around that part of town and found it drab. Certainly, the crumbling colonial facades had some character but this was dispelled by a backcloth of dreary concrete apartment blocks.

The business of understanding and being understood by someone who spoke no English was a pantomime in itself. The accommodation was awful and smelly but he had known worse – though only in the 'nick'.

Bill took him to lunch, however, and also introduced Ronnie to his friends. One was a young clerk called Andanto at the American Express office who could speak English. A mutual love of jazz led to an offer to show Mr Haynes the town, which was enthusiastically accepted. Their night out had the added bonus of securing the Amex office as a *poste restante* address.

Another friend of Bill's was a widowed lady called Nadine, a committed Christian Scientist. While others introduced Ronnie to clubs and the joys of marijuana, Nadine invited him to church. Shrewd enough to latch on to the invitation, he soon met yet more new friends, in particular a wealthy Swiss couple, the Blumers, who, learning of his carpentry skills, offered to employ him to work at their house.

The Blumers in turn introduced him to other rich friends and Ronnie soon had his feet well under the table. By the time six months had elapsed, he had acquired a home, a freelance occupation, a girlfriend and a social circle.

His comfortable lifestyle was disturbed only by the need to renew his visa. The easiest way to do this, to avoid answering awkward questions, was to cross the border into an adjoining country and to return on a new and automatic tourist visa. He needed to do this to keep his passport in order so that at some stage he could return to Australia.

One day a letter arrived, via his friend at the Amex office.

He read it then and there, out in the street. The very first words advised him to sit down before he read on. He had already flash permutated a number of shocks in his mind – but not the one that was coming. His oldest son, Nicky, had been killed in a car crash. Charmian had been driving but was not at fault. Farley had also been injured, though not seriously. Charmian and Chris had been severely shocked but were now recovered.

Traumatised, Biggs felt his world had come to an end, as if this were some kind of cruel punishment for his sins. Eyes blinded with tears, he staggered into a bar and ordered consecutive brandies. His head spinning, all he could think of to do at that moment was to give himself up at the British Consulate, as though this would in some way make amends to Charmian and the other boys.

He thought to go back to Australia but his visa had almost expired and needed to be renewed immediately for him to use Mike Haynes' passport. To do this he went to Bolivia, another uncomfortable journey, but within a week was back in Rio, to the new apartment that had been found for him at Botafogo Beach.

His new apartment brought back all the happy memories of Rio, as did the loving and sympathetic greeting from his girlfriend Edith. He knew he could never forget the shock of learning about Nicky's death. It would scar him for life but the wound, like all wounds, would heal. On reflection, his first reaction, to leave Rio, seemed a foolish one. Charmian would be all right, their friends would take good care of her.

For the time being, there was no point in taking risks. His visa had been renewed and life was good – and safe – in Rio. He decided to stay.

Ronnie Biggs was always a pragmatist.

In the months that followed, he corresponded with Charmian, deploring their loss but claiming that his return would merely unsettle the other two boys. She, well aware in her own mind of his infidelities, replied that he was just getting cold feet.

In fact he was living it up to the strains of the samba in the various clubs where he was now a regular visitor, especially when Edith was away, as she then was. And it was in one of these clubs, the Bola Oreta, that he met a young Brazilian dancer and promptly began yet another affair.

Raimunda Nascimiento de Castro, nicknamed Xiu-Xiu, would come to play a very important part in the continuing saga of Ronnie Biggs' adventures and escapades.

* * *

Ronnie enjoyed a brief fling with Raimunda while still continuing his long-term affair with Edith. Both of them had keys to his apartment, as did one or two others.

He obviously liked playing with fire and came very close to getting his fingers burned on more than one occasion. Taking the pragmatic course, as ever, though with considerable regret, he dumped tempestuous Raimunda in favour of the pliable and financially reliable Edith.

He worked hard whenever he could, though always remaining dependent on Edith to see him through, and played hard whenever he could, his life being an endless round of eating, drinking, enjoying music and girls, and smoking dope. Already he was a quite well known figure among the clubs, bars and restaurants of Rio.

Every so often, Edith would take time off to go to New York to see her sister, occasions when Ronnie would re-ignite the affair, but he was far too shrewd to exchange the dependable Edith for the volatile Raimunda, though he had thought about it. The decision as to which he should choose was, in the end, made for him. Without anyone knowing, Edith had met and married a German in New York, where she now intended to live.

There were no hard feelings as far as Ronnie was concerned. As soon as Edith left for New York, Raimunda moved herself into the apartment.

In 1973 Ronnie met a young man named Constantine Benckendorff, known as Conti, to whom he confided his real identity. It was a confidence he had shared fairly widely by now: he was confident the British authorities could not touch him in Brazil.

All of these factors contributed to Biggs' next plan. By now a parole system was in force in the United Kingdom and some of those who had been convicted along with Biggs might well be released within the next year or two.

He felt very isolated and, not for the first time, his thoughts turned to giving himself up. He would still have to serve time but would, at some time in the future, be free at last. His hope was that, by surrendering to the law, any sentence he received would be reduced in recognition of that.

The more he thought about the scheme, the more possibilities it seemed to have. He was well aware of his own publicity value and the story of his voluntarily returning to gaol would be front-page news.

Many people had made a few quid because of some peripheral connection to the train robbers, including Charmian, whose deal with Kerry Packer had financed the escape to Rio. If he could organise it properly, he could raise sufficient funds to look after both Charmian and Raimunda, while allowing him a last riotous hurrah.

He road-tested the plan on his new friend, Constantine, who thought he was mad even to think about it but, nevertheless, agreed to help. Conti was going to London in December 1973 and, at Biggs' request, would probe delicately to see whether any of the national newspapers would be interested in covering the story.

Conti did not have to look far; a contact introduced him to the *Daily Express*, who jumped at the idea. They were wary of being conned however, having burnt their fingers on a hoax concerning Martin Bormann, Hitler's deputy, also alleged to be a fugitive in South America. But when a reporter named Colin McKenzie, on behalf of the *Express*, telephoned Biggs early in the year of 1974, the train robber was only too pleased to furnish proof of his identity, including a jaunty note in his own handwriting and a set of fingerprints. Convinced, the *Express* agreed a fee of £35,000*, which itself was the amount of a reasonable mail-train robbery, plus expenses, to have an exclusive of Biggs' voluntary return to England to give himself up. The last of the Great Train Robbers, courtesy of the *Daily Express* – it would be a sensation!

And after all, Biggs probably reasoned, once the paper had sent its reporters to Rio, interviewed and photographed him,

* worth £350,000 today

and more importantly paid him the money, he could always have second thoughts about actually returning.

He was, and always would be, a slippery customer.

As it happened, he never actually had to make that decision because events were going to take another turn altogether. At first, however, everything went strictly to plan.

The *Daily Express* men arrived, Colin McKenzie, who was to conduct the interview, and Bill Lovelace, a photographer. Money changed hands immediately and the ever-generous Ronnie, when flush, was eager to show them Rio's exotic night-life. Most curiously for a pair of journalists, however, they cried off, citing tiredness and generally feeling under the weather. McKenzie also stressed the fact that they were not here on holiday. They would need at least two or three days to tape Ronnie's story of his stay in Rio, how he had managed to evade the law for so long, and what had driven him to give himself up. There were also the necessary travel arrangements to fix up and preparations to be made for his dramatic arrival in the UK, all organised by the *Daily Express*.

Ronnie made the most of his last few days of freedom, eating, drinking and smoking pot to excess. He turned up for work quite consistently however, both for his interviews and for various set poses for the photographer, usually with bikini-clad beauties. His life in Brazil had been a riot and the *Express* wanted to record it all faithfully – perhaps even to show what the 'reformed' criminal was giving up in order to seek redemption.

Ronnie did not care, all he wanted was the money. Today he was due to finalise his story. It was going to be a momentous day in every respect.

It started badly, true, when Raimunda announced that she was pregnant, but this had happened before and she had a friend who was a nurse, who could arrange a termination. In any case, Ronnie had made sure that the bulk of the money from the *Daily Express* deal would go both to Charmian and to

Raimunda, so that they would be looked after. Or had he been so generous in order to convince the *Daily Express* that he really wanted to give himself up?

Whatever he had in mind, it didn't work out – not in the way he expected anyhow.

SLIPPER SLIPS UP

It was the first day of February 1974. The *Daily Express* team had booked a suite at the Trocadero, which served as a general office for their activities.

Ronnie had arrived for a day's tape-recording with McKenzie. Lovelace was on hand, cameras at the ready. They had roped in the beautiful Lucia – who was Biggs' lover when Raimunda was not around – for the photo-shoot. She was naked apart from the most minimal of bikinis and Conti, who was acting as gofer, was slavering over her as Bill arranged suitably provocative poses. Also included was Ronnie, stripped off apart from his swimming trunks.

As soon as the session was over, just as Ronnie was just about to change into his shirt and slacks, the doorbell rang. He assumed it was room service, summoned by the *Express* boys in their customary generous and hospitable fashion. Conti went to open the door and found himself shoved back into the room by the tall, commanding figure of Superintendent Jack Slipper, head of the Metropolitan Flying Squad. Ronnie recognised him instantly but could think of nothing to mark the policeman's arrival other than 'Oh, fuck!'

With Slipper was another policeman, Detective Inspector Peter Jones, as well as the British Consul, Henry Neill. He was accompanied by his Brazilian Vice-Consul and two plain-clothes policemen.

Biggs was taken aback and mortified. For years he had

dreamed and had nightmares about this moment, yet, now it had come, it was totally unexpected. What had happened? McKenzie and Lovelace had both seemed as stunned as Ronnie by Slipper's dramatic entrance but it clearly could not be entirely a coincidence that they were all there at the same time.

If the men from the *Express* were not themselves culpable, then their bosses must have been. After all, they had their story now in words and pictures: it made little difference to them whether Biggs was arrested when arriving at Heathrow to give himself up, or in Rio by Slipper of the Yard – in fact, the latter was probably a better story.

It was a double-cross worthy of the criminal classes, although they would probably have deplored it as dishonourable. As far as Ronnie was concerned this was grand larceny. He had received only a fraction of the agreed sum as an advance and he doubted whether he would now see another penny. The grandstand climax to his criminal career, as he had pictured it and sold it to the *Express*, was now one of ignominious failure. The very idea made him plead with Slipper not to be taken in handcuffs.

There was much jabbering in Portuguese as the dialogue was reported to the local police and, as if to make it clear that Ronnie would be no trouble to them, handcuffed or not, one of them showed off the gun stuck in his belt.

Slipper was satisfied his entourage could cope but still took a firm hold of the back of Ronnie's belt as he was taken out to the elevator. McKenzie, Lucia and Conti were left in the hotel room but Bill Lovelace had somehow sneaked out and, in true *Express* style, was then waiting, cameras at the ready, as Biggs and his accompanying posse left the hotel and moved to the waiting cars.

The old Catete Palace, a former presidential residence, was at that time being used by the Brazilian federal police as their headquarters in Rio. The cigar-chomping *delegado*, or police chief, was one Carlos Alberto Garcia.

The Scotland Yard men may have entered the Trocadero Hotel like gang-busters but Garcia was not impressed by their attitude when they brought Biggs to him. The story they told was a curious one, that the Michael John Haynes they had brought in was the subject of an extradition order regarding unpaid child support. Biggs had been told to go along with this in order to give the arrest as low a profile as possible. Otherwise, Slipper had hinted darkly, they would hand him over to the Brazilian secret police, who would probably torture him and then throw his body into the sea from a military aeroplane.

Jack Slipper may have had his own ideas about the way the Brazilian police acted but they did not coincide with those of Garcia, who was not too pleased about the way the man from Scotland Yard had entered his office and was laying down the law.

Biggs meanwhile had been taken into custody, with more than a little trepidation, for Brazilian gaols had a grisly reputation, but was allowed a visit by the Consul. Henry Neill explained to him that it would not be a good idea for him to admit that he had entered the country on a forged passport, since this would bring an automatic gaol sentence – out here, a decidedly unpleasant experience – before being deported to resume his stay at Wandsworth. He was told to say quite simply that he had crossed one of the borders without a passport.

That unfortunately kicked off a whole bureaucratic process involving sets of fingerprints, which, as a matter of routine, were checked against the files from Interpol relating to wanted criminals. Carlos Garcia was unperturbed by these delays but Slipper and Jones – and especially Slipper – were getting distinctly 'shirty'. For them, time was of the essence: they had a flight booked for their return to England and had already arranged a celebratory dinner to mark the crowning achievement of Slipper's distinguished career.

Alas, the *delegado* was in no such hurry and was becoming

increasingly offended by the Detective Superintendent's hectoring. Carlos Garcia was a man who liked to be always correct: there is a protocol in these matters and a courtesy to be observed. The headquarters of the Brazilian federal police in Rio de Janeiro was not to be taken for some provincial British police station. Garcia never forgot this confrontation with Slipper and his recollections of the incident are extraordinary.

'He is my prisoner!' was an unfortunate phrase to cross Slipper's lips, and banging on Garcia's desk as a forceful accompaniment was even more of a mistake. From the beginning Garcia had thought Jack Slipper was taking this arrest far too personally: he had come across policemen with obsessions before and, while these obsessions perhaps made good stories for the movies, in his own experience they were counter-productive.

Since the banging of fists and the raised voices were getting a bit too much for him, he coolly ordered the two British policemen to be restrained by handcuffing them behind their backs. He warned them they had no jurisdiction in his country and they were only being entertained in federal headquarters as a courtesy. On the facts as known by him, he advised them, they had arrested a resident of Brazil without authority and then detained him – it was in effect a kidnapping!

Leaving the spluttering Slipper and his fellow kidnapper to spend some time cooling down, Garcia went off to interview Mr Haynes himself. By this time the Interpol enquiry had identified Michael Haynes' fingerprints as being those of Ronald Biggs, escaped train robber. Biggs made no effort to deny it. Seemingly relieved that the truth was out, he confessed everything and recanted the explanation he had given previously as a story he had been instructed to tell by Slipper.

If the British police had been in trouble before, they were now really in it. Garcia ordered them to be released from their handcuffs and told them they were free to leave – but without

Biggs! Garcia even lectured the Scotland Yard superintendent: Biggs was not 'his' prisoner but a prisoner of the justice system. Garcia himself could not decide the outcome, he said. That was a matter for his superiors in Brasilia, the capital city.

The British pair could stay or leave as they wished. No doubt the matter of extradition would be considered but he doubted whether there would be any immediate decision. In the meantime, Biggs would be held in safe custody, in prison.

For three days Slipper and Jones were forced to hang around, getting increasingly impatient. Matters of extradition, it was slyly pointed out to them, needed to be delicately handled. Slipper was reminded of extradition requests made by the Brazilians to the British government, in respect of political subversives known to be living in the UK, refused on the basis that they had been granted asylum. It began to look as though their gung-ho attempt to arrest Ronnie Biggs and make a prompt return with him to the UK was doomed to fail.

THE THIRD GREAT ESCAPE

Meanwhile, Ronnie Biggs, accustomed though he was to detention, was finding hospitality in a Brazilian gaol hard to take. His three cell mates were friendly, however, and honoured by the presence of one of the famous great train robbers.

Biggs told them how happy he had been during his four years in Brazil and how he had worked hard and kept his nose clean. He had a beautiful girlfriend who only that day had announced that she was pregnant, he said, playing for sympathy and omitting the abortion he had suggested. On hearing the news, Mario went into ecstasies. A taxi driver by trade, his many encounters with the law had made him something of a legal expert: if Biggs had fathered a Brazilian child he would never be made to leave. Mario, knowingly or not, had fired a rocket, a Very light that illuminated all Biggs' horizons: was there really a chance of escape?

Without hesitation he asked permission from the gaol authorities to allow him a visit from his common-law wife, praying she had not yet had time to do anything about the unwanted child which was now, suddenly, desperately wanted: Ronnie Biggs' paternal instincts had never been stronger.

His request, backed by the Consul, was granted, and Ronnie was returned, suitably restrained, to the federal offices where Neill and Slipper were making their regular daily visits – the latter still making peremptory, if guarded, demands which washed like water off a duck's back. Garcia's reply was simply that when he knew, he would let them know, and that was the end of it. In fact, the *delegado*'s attention had already turned to other matters.

The *delegado* had taken note of the attractive young woman who was in his outer office, waiting for Biggs to arrive, and he could not fail to be moved by the torrent of tears that she shed as she saw her man, handcuffed, arrive at the *delegacia*. Ever gallant, he put his arm around the weeping girl and soothed her by saying he would do all he could to help. He did not say, but meant, that he would do all he could to give Jack Slipper one in the eye.

Watching the scene of tender reconciliation, it occurred to the *delegado*, who had always had a fondness for the dramatic, that the story of the escaped train robber and his love for a poor Brazilian girl would make a splendid item for *Fantastico*! This was Brazil's most popular programme, a peculiar concoction of news and views from around the world interspersed with items of light entertainment.

It is a matter of judgement in which category the Biggs segment fell but the public took to it hook, line and sinker. As Garcia saw it, this was good publicity for his department, showing the ill-fated couple expressing their undying love for each other in his office, and he got a fairly handsome fee for making the arrangements, as well as realising a life-long ambition, to direct for television.

For Biggs it was a red-letter day. Raimunda had confirmed that she was still pregnant and he had begged her with tears in his eyes to have the child, their child. So long as she named him as the father, the infant could be his passport to freedom

The following day there was enormous press, radio and television coverage with the Brazilian public reacting in a storm of indignation at this neo-colonial attempt at abduction of the father of a Brazilian child – all of it received with much good-humoured back-slapping and cursing by Mario and the other occupants of Ronnie's cell.

Jack Slipper and Peter Jones watched the show on TV with total abhorrence and then the next day learned that Brasilia had decided to detain Biggs for a further ninety days while they considered whether they would make an expulsion order.

Slipper was not holding his breath on that one and he and Jones got the first plane out of that hell-hole that Rio had become, disgusted with their treatment.

Though he had given no interviews, to rub it in, the world's press had converged on Rio to witness his discomfiture. On the plane home, Slipper and Jones sat side by side. When Jones went off to the toilet, an astute photographer snapped Jack Slipper and the empty seat next to him, with the implication that the seat had been reserved for master-criminal Ronnie Biggs. Slipper had failed, the Superintendent had come back without his man. He had become a laughing stock. His high-handed attempt to extradite Biggs, or kidnap him as Garcia had characterised it, had backfired. It should have been Jack Slipper as the hero of the hour. Instead it was Biggs, in the public's perception anyway.

Poor old Jack Slipper had been left looking pretty stupid and, forever thereafter, would endure the *sobriquet* 'Slip-up'.

Slipper's superior officer, Sir Robert Mark, the Metropolitan Police Commissioner, would in due course be forced by the Home Office to write a grovelling and apologetic letter to the Chief of Brazilian Police regarding the Slipper incident.

Ronnie Biggs was sent back to gaol while the authorities in Brasilia decided his fate. A fellow prisoner was a French con-artist called Fernand Legros, who took Ronnie under his wing. A smooth talker, he also impressed Raimunda with his suave personality, even volunteering to be godfather to the unborn child.

Jack Slipper was the butt of most of the world's press and, soon enough, the journalists came calling at Charmian's house. She was shocked, not so much by the girlfriend – she had always expected him to have affairs – but because he was to become a father again. It explained a lot: why he had been so reluctant to return to Australia and why she had heard so little from him recently.

For years she had been faithful to him, wanting only to restart their lives together, whatever it cost. She desperately needed to know now from him, directly, whether they still had a future. The money from the robbery had almost expired but the press again came to her aid, offering to finance a trip to South America for her and the children, in return for the story and pictures.

In her own mind she had already determined her position. If Ronnie had really been ready to go back to the UK to give himself up – which she very much doubted – then she too, though she had learned to love Australia, would be ready to return home with the boys and wait until they could be re-united again as a family.

On the other hand, he had now found a safe haven in Brazil, it being dependent on the child he had fathered: Charmian would understand if he wanted to marry the woman and she would give him his freedom.

It certainly broke the monotony of Biggs' detention to be visited by his wife, as well as Raimunda, whom Charmian dubbed his Indian whore. Ronnie, as always, wanted to compromise, make the best of the situation.

Although the *Daily Express* had apparently welched on their deal, McKenzie had come up with another to replace it. A huge advance from a publisher for a book was on its way. His release was imminent, or so he had been told, and he needed McKenzie to obtain the funds with which to look after both Raimunda and the other Biggs family, while he made up his mind what to do.

There was probably never ever any doubt in his mind. Brazil, in his view, was no place for Charmian or the boys, who loved Australia anyway. And for Ronnie there was no other place to live: the child would be his passport to quasi-citizenship.

He had money at last and there was the prospect of much more in the future. He was now, thanks to the Brazilian government, openly a celebrity. Raimunda's part in the drama had made her a minor celebrity too, much to her delight. And their child-to-be – who, she assured him, would be a son – was already marked out for stardom.

Fernand Legros, the con-man and putative godfather, had been deported to France from where he promised Raimunda a ceremony akin to a coronation, and she was thrilled by the idea of visiting Europe.

Biggs was returned to the *delegacia* in Rio on May 6th and conditionally released the next day. Charmian, courtesy of the Australian newspapers, revisited Brazil. Ronnie balanced his life precariously, spending the days with his family and the nights with Raimunda.

It was never going to work out. Charmian returned with the boys to the place that was now their home. En route she visited England to see her mother. Her parents had distanced themselves from her since the time she took up with Biggs, who was always a cheap crook in their eyes. Her father sadly had died before any reconciliation could take place. Charmian knew he would only have said, 'I told you so', and he would have been right.

On August 16th 1974, Michael Fernand Nascimiento de Castro Biggs was born and Ronnie was free at last.

PART
TWO

What happened…

SEX PISTOLS

Public opinion is fickle. While the world had applauded Biggs for yet another audacious escape, eventually there was a backlash.

The other train robbers had served their time, paid their debt to society, while Ronnie continued to whoop it up in Rio, making large sums from the enormous publicity he and Raimunda had created. In 1975, Roy James was the first of the men sentenced to thirty years to be released. Biggs would probably have been released by now as well. In the same year Buster Edwards and Jimmy White were let go, followed by Jim Hussey and Gordon Goody.

While Raimunda was visiting Europe with little Michael as guests of his godfather, Fernand Legros, Ronnie had plenty of time to think of what might have been. Fernand Legros had been a generous host and Raimunda was soon to return to Paris. Legros had taken her under his wing there and she had, with his assistance, carved out a career for herself as an 'exotic dancer' – in other words, a stripper, the moll of a famous gangster. There was more money made, by all the parties concerned, from publicity attached to the Great Train Robbery, than there had been from the heist itself.

Biggs strove to keep himself in the public eye. He conned a few grand out of a group planning yet another book, this time attributing the Great Train Robbery to a German mastermind, none other than war hero Colonel Otto Scorzeny, who had rescued Mussolini. He thought he was onto a money spinner when the Sex Pistols visited Brazil and enthusiastically joined the group for a song especially written for them, rather heartlessly entitled 'Cosh the Driver', but in Malcolm McLaren he found someone too smart for him. Although the record sold millions, Biggs claimed he never received a penny in royalties.

There was an incident when a group of British sailors, whose ship was visiting Rio, came across Biggs and after some hours of riotous drinking took him back to HMS *Danae* where technically he was on British territory. He had not been taken prisoner however, and the incident made a great story for the newspapers – only the officer in charge being reprimanded.

Although nominally free, Ronnie Biggs was actually a prisoner in Rio. He had to report at first weekly and then fortnightly to the police. He was not allowed to work officially and, apart from a few small private jobs, soon found he had to scrape a living from tourists who paid to have their photographs taken with him. Large sums had passed through his hands but, with Ronnie, money could never stick.

He wanted out but there was no way out. He had little money and his habits of drink and drugs were becoming expensive. The Rio police heard rumours that their celebrity visitor wanted to enter the lucrative Brazilian narcotics trade. He thought that by using his old criminal contacts he could start a drugs route to Britain and Continental Europe. After all, he reasoned, ex train robber Charlie Wilson, now released, was already smuggling drugs into Spain and doing well. But Biggs' foray into the narcotics business faltered before it started, not by police action but by the local drugs barons who reckoned his celebrity status would be dangerous and attract too much attention. All Ronnie was left with were tourists: he was like an exhibit in a freak show. It was a depressing thought and, the more depressed he got, the more he turned to stimulants. It was a downward spiral.

* * *

On the other side of the Atlantic, another man, one who was to play a major role in the Ronnie Biggs drama, had a very different attitude to life. John Miller was born in Motherwell, Scotland, in 1945. By the time he was eighteen he had joined the Scots Guards, one of the elite regiments in the British Army. At six foot two, he kept himself fit and was a fine athlete. He joined the regimental boxing team, as a light heavyweight, where he met Londoner Fred Prime, a man who was to become a life-long friend.

Initially John enjoyed army life, seeing active service in Malaya and Borneo. The Guards regiments, however, are based for much of the time in London, where they carry out public duties such as changing the guard at Buckingham Palace. For a young Scots soldier, London was a treasure trove of fun and excitement, especially Soho, then the capital's red light district.

Leaving the army briefly in the early Seventies, Miller tried his luck on Civvie Street. Unfortunately he was lured by a bad crowd back into Soho and, before he knew it, he was being charged and convicted for minor pornography offences and subsequently fined. Making a tactical retreat from Soho, he rejoined the Army, promising himself that next time he got out he would be better prepared.

John Miller was fascinated by the world of popular music, and he guessed that his best entry into that world was through the security business. Rock groups attracted not only groupies but fans in their thousands, whose presence in such numbers could be dangerous. There was also a lunatic fringe – nutters who could be intimidating, even homicidal. Top grade security was essential for any band's continuing success and this was the field of endeavour chosen by John Miller.

On his discharge in 1976, he found himself in the right place at the right time when the punk revolution hit town. Helping out at a club called the Vortex in Wardour Street, he looked after 'names' like Billy Idol, Annie Lennox and the Sex Pistols, and from that base started to work with bands like the

Bay City Rollers, doing security or as business manager. He also worked for a while at Richard Branson's Venue club.

But things were slow, profits were not rolling in as Miller had hoped they would. However, he knew he had been born blessed with one precious talent, what Londoners call 'the gift of the gab'. He had the ability to talk people into things, to think on his feet. He had a fertile imagination and always believed being outrageous would carve for him a way forward in life. Fred Prime, his fellow Guardsman, would say, 'John can con anybody into anything. He can talk the hind legs off a donkey.'

Miller's big break came when he befriended millionaire playboy Stephen Bentinck, convincing him that he needed personal security. Miller called his new company Executive Security and Bentinck became his first client. For whatever reason, Bentinck took a liking to John and, particularly, Fred Prime. Both enjoyed themselves at his expense, even visiting the family's twenty thousand acre ranch in northern California on a 'jolly'.

It is a tradition among British soldiers to nickname everyone. Fred soon affectionately christened Bentinck 'Snaky' after seeing him staggering out of the bathroom of his apartment, stark naked after a night on the town.

Being constantly around the rich and impressionable 'Snaky' was an opportunity not wasted by Miller. Using his considerable persuasive powers, he convinced the young playboy to back the new security company. Bentinck gave Miller the use of a small office in Soho's Greek Street, rent free, and a promise of some money to promote the company.

Miller was on a roll and wanted to hit the big time fast. For some time he had been planning to go to Rio de Janeiro, Brazil, to take a look at Maracana Stadium where the big British bands performed. Brazil was also famous of course for harbouring Ronnie Biggs, Britain's most wanted fugitive, which prompted Miller to have a brainwave. If he could kidnap Biggs, that would result in huge publicity, not only for his fledgling company but himself.

He confided his idea to Fred Prime and another ex-Scots Guardsman who had joined the company, former boxer Norrie Boyle.

'Rio's a great place. Bands like Queen and The Who are going there,' John told them. 'We can see what security work is going. And get Ronnie Biggs.'

Fred laughed, thinking John was joking. 'Here we go again,' he said.

GOODBYE, MR BOND

In April 1979 John Miller and Fred Prime flew to Rio for what, as soldiers, they called a 'recce'. Miller warned Fred not to breathe a word to Snaky about the real reason for their trip. After ten days they flew back to London, armed with enough information about Biggs' whereabouts to formulate a kidnap plan.

Miller's plan was for Fred, Norrie and himself to pose as a second unit film crew for the new James Bond movie, *Moonraker*, currently being filmed in Brazil. They would offer Biggs a cameo part, enticing him with an offer of five thousand for a day's work. Biggs' part would simply involve his having to board a yacht in Rio and then sail round the harbour, all of which would be filmed. In fact, what would really happen once Biggs was on board was that the yacht would keep sailing.

Miller figured they would need between fifteen and twenty thousand pounds. Bentinck, not knowing what Miller really wanted, was only trickling comparatively small amounts through to the company, nowhere near Miller's needs to carry out his stunt. So privately Miller made the rounds of some of London's wealthier residents, including Richard Branson, boss of Virgin Airlines, to raise cash. 'I firmly turned him down,' Branson was to write in a letter to the *Sunday Times* after the fiasco, as he called it, was over. Miller also failed to extract money from a film producer named Christopher Raphael, whom he had cornered in a South Kensington discotheque.

In the haunts that Miller frequented, he began to get a reputation as a man obsessed with kidnapping Ronnie Biggs, but nobody took him seriously. In the end it was decided to get Bentinck to pay, even if he didn't know it.

The more Miller considered the mooted adventure, the more he liked it: this time he would really hit the headlines. To make sure of this, he outlined the whole kidnap plan, even before it happened, to a friend, Gavin Goodwin. Goodwin was a newspaper reporter from Glasgow who had written a story a decade earlier about Miller's time working as a cowboy in Guyana. Miller could always spin adventurous tales about his experiences.

The story was told to Goodwin in the strictest confidence, revealing the streak of naivety that sometimes belied Miller's hard-man persona. Journalists might not reveal their sources but they do talk to other journalists. It was to be a costly mistake.

It was not too difficult to track down the escaped criminal, who by then was living in a house in Sepitiba, just outside Rio, with Michael, his son, and Raimunda, whenever she showed up. Fidelity had never been Ronnie's strong suit and her absences did not bother him, allowing him to start up other non-exclusive relationships.

Although he had worked hard as a carpenter during his time in Australia and when he first came to Brazil, he was bound by the conditions of his release not to work in Rio. Much as he may have been tempted, he dared not risk indulging in any criminal activities, which meant that the only way he had of earning a living was by exploiting his own notoriety, a kind of busking. He granted interviews, posed for pictures with tourists, allowed himself to be used in any damn-fool publicity stunts, just about anything that could turn a buck that was cash in hand. As the excitement of having a great train robber as a resident began to fade away for the public, he became increasingly desperate to cash in on any scheme that would reward his services.

Ronnie saw himself as something of a star, although he had not yet graduated to the silver screen, so it can be imagined that when he met John Miller and his friends, posing as a crew of stunt men on the new James Bond epic which was currently filming in Brazil, he thought that maybe his big chance had come.

The tall, powerfully-built man who introduced himself as John Miller told Ronnie that he had served in the Scots Guards before finding work in the movie business.

The three men rapidly insinuated themselves into Biggs' social circle, such as it was, even becoming friends with the four-year-old Michael Biggs. Miller was a charming and amusing companion, with a host of picaresque stories, while Fred Prime, the strong man of the group, rapidly acquired a dog-like affection for the train robber with whom he shared a South London upbringing. Norrie was great fun too, a real prankster. He had taken a shine to young Michael, who found the gang's antics hilarious – he called them crazy men.

Before leaving, Miller had tried to hire an ocean-going yacht to come and pick them up, but without much success. Most charter yachts were based in the Caribbean, approximately twelve days sailing from Rio. The best that Nicholson Yacht Charters of Cambridge, Massachusetts could do was a seventy foot yacht called *Ocean Scorpio*, moored in Barbados. The snag, however, was it had to return there within three weeks and that would not be long enough for them to get to Rio and back, so it was suggested instead that John's film crew could fly to the port of Belem in northern Brazil. That would save seven days' sailing and there would be no problem. There would be enough time to fit everything in with their schedule.

Where the hell was Belem? Nobody had ever heard of it. Anyway, a quick look at the map and the decision was made, there being no other option if they were to go ahead. The hire would be $6,000 per week, and a deposit of $10,000 was wired to Nicholson's to secure the vessel, without even seeing it or knowing who the skipper was.

With this change of plan, Miller reckoned they would now have to leave Ronnie in Barbados from where he could be extradited to the United Kingdom. He also concocted a new story. He explained that Lewis Gilbert, the director of the Bond film, would love to have Ronnie play a guest role, but Ronnie had to understand the director could not shift the whole, massive crew to Rio, since that would be inordinately expensive. Miller suggested a possible compromise, that the scenes the director had in mind could be shot on the south coast, where the production was on location, and he was prepared to put this to Lewis Gilbert. He knew Ronnie was too shrewd to risk moving outside Brazil. In fact, Ronnie did not even want to venture outside Rio and, anyway, the terms of his conditional release forbade it.

Shrugging away objections, Miller and company continued to lavish hospitality on Mike and Ronnie – and his friends – with the big Scotsman forever selling Ronnie the idea of hopping on a plane at the local Santos Dumont Airport to go south and, for just a few days' away, to earn five thousand pounds.

Ronnie was tempted.

Miller's two friends had similar backgrounds. Norrie Boyle was also an ex-Guardsman, a former colour sergeant, and Fred Prime had been a former regular soldier with the Scots Guards.

Fred, like the others, was built like an outhouse and had been a British army boxing champion, who had once knocked out Idi Amin, the brutish President of Uganda, when the African was just an NCO. Fred had also been a sparring partner for the great Mohammed Ali (then Cassius Clay) when he came to England to fight and beat Henry Cooper, the British heavyweight champion. Fred, unlike his companions, was a South Londoner whose familiar Cockney dialect endeared him to Ronnie immediately: the two soon struck up a rapport.

Ronnie's new-found pals were great companions, formidable drinkers, wonderful storytellers – and they had money to burn. Perhaps that was why Ronnie never thought twice about the coincidence of these three burly ex-servicemen working together in the film industry, a business that was notoriously difficult to get into, controlled as it then was by a union that rigorously administered a tightly restrictive closed shop. But then, his only previous experience of film was with Malcolm McLaren, manager of the Sex Pistols, who produced the aptly named documentary *The Great Rock and Roll Swindle*.

Whether Ronnie was being completely foolhardy or playing a cunning game of his own, it was difficult to tell: probably the latter. One thing is certain: he did not intend to relinquish the opportunity to make a few thousand pounds easily.

He continued to play the game, agreeing in principle, or from lack of it, to take the risk of leaving Rio for a couple of days, for five thousand pounds down, cash in hand, with more to come after he had finished his 'work'.

Two seasoned opportunists played out a game of wits. Miller went through the pantomime of contacting Lewis Gilbert, who was not even in Brazil at the time, and then came back with the offer of two thousand pounds, in cash. The situation was neatly balanced.

Ronnie's mind was made up by yet another telephone call he received that night, this time from the *Daily Star*, a reporter called Bullet McCartney with some good connections in Rio. He told Ronnie that some 'Jock reporter' was in London claiming he knew of an intended kidnap by some Scottish ex-Guardsmen, and the paper was taking the information sufficiently seriously to hold back several pages in case the story broke. Miller had certainly achieved his aim of getting enormous press interest, so long as he could capitalise on it.

With courage, or foolhardiness – or perhaps because he was just desperate for 'readies' – Biggs decided he would blag the two thousand pounds and then put as much distance as possible between himself and the charismatic, though probably dangerous, Scotsman and his heavyweight friends.

A last supper – or lunch anyway – was arranged at the Copacabana Hotel where the gang was staying. Since Miller was to be the host, Ronnie, never one to do things by half, had invited all his friends and told them to bring their friends. He was determined to make sure that this would be a very expensive scam.

Among Ronnie's invitees were Big Joe, an all-in wrestler, and Armin Heim, a burly German ex-paratrooper, both of whom had been tipped off that there might be trouble. Ronnie could not imagine that anyone would grab him in the Copacabana, in broad daylight, but he was taking no chances: he had even told Armin Heim, who was now a photographer, to get snaps of the three conspirators.

The more likely plan of course was to get him to Santos Dumont Airport and then fly him somewhere else, but he was not going to risk that happening. In the end, a telephone call a friend had made to London confirmed all his suspicions – Lewis Gilbert was not in Brazil, nor intending to be since all shooting there had been concluded. That was it. Ronnie decided to attend the party, since that was the best way to ensure the would-be kidnappers were all in place and then, uncharacteristically, call the police!

He had a perfect excuse: it was his day for signing on at the local police station – a weekly routine. The gang knew that. He was still hoping to blag Miller out of the two grand but the Scotsman was far too canny to hand over money until Ronnie was ready to travel. It was not a time to take chances. He slipped quietly away from the party to do what had to be done. Win some, lose some, had always been his philosophy.

He could see now how much money the Scot must have planned to earn from all the publicity. Indeed he felt there would still be a story there and hoped to be able to make some money out of it for himself: by now he was fully attuned to the wages accrued from newspaper stories.

After signing on, he asked to see the new *delegado*, Dr Pitta, and told him the whole story as he knew it. Dr Pitta was most offended that such shenanigans were being planned on his territory.

The lunch party was still boozily under way when Miller discovered that Ronnie had skipped, and he soon knew where. Undeterred, he went himself to the police station where he waited across the road for Ronnie to come out. Instead, the police came out for him.

Miller was questioned for some hours, while other agents went in search of Fred and Norrie, who had checked out of the Copacabana and into a small hotel adjacent to the Santos Dumont Airport.

While they were looking, the silver-tongued Miller was explaining how Biggs had been trying to con them out of some cash and, when he was refused, had reported them as an act of vindictiveness: it was all a cock-and-bull story.

Pitta agreed but he was referring to Miller's account. The police chief remembered well enough the attempts of the British police to snatch Biggs, ahead of the granting of any extradition order – which in any case had been denied. He had no intention of releasing Miller until the men searching for Fred Prime and Norrie Boyle had reported back.

They had found the two ex-soldiers and brought them back for questioning. Fred, under strict orders from Miller, was saying nothing. Boyle on the other hand, apprehensive about possible detention in a Brazilian gaol, said he was prepared to make a statement – at which point he was immediately knocked cold by Prime, who announced that no one was making any statements. It took the intervention of five policemen to restrain Fred, who was lucky that the only damage he had inflicted was on his own colleague.

Dr Pitta carefully studied the passports of the three men, all of which stated under Occupation: 'Government Service'. In fact, this was simply because, when the passports were issued, all were still serving soldiers. The police chief found the entries somewhat sinister however, and decided to refer matters upwards.

The Brazilians had suffered one bruising international scandal – the Jack Slipper incident – and they did not want another. Regardless of what theories they could speculate on concerning the involvement of the British government, no crime had taken place. The men were an embarrassment and were ordered to leave the country immediately. The *Ocean Scorpio* was still waiting for them in Belem, ready to sail. The police suggested they should do so without delay – and made sure they did.

For Ronnie it was another astonishing escape to add to all the others in his ten years of freedom so far. He was rapidly gaining the reputation as a latter-day Houdini.

The game, however, was not over yet. There were other interested parties mulling over his escape, drawing the conclusion that it was not so much Ronnie's shrewdness or good luck that had saved him but rather, perhaps, that Miller, though an outstanding operative, also loved publicity too much for his own good.

There was no reason why, some people thought, an attempt should not be made again, when the dust had settled.

THE KIDNAP GAME

On his return to Britain, John Miller got his publicity. Although two major British tabloids, the *Sun* and the *Daily Star*, ran stories about Miller's attempt to kidnap Biggs, the event was portrayed as a complete fiasco. It wasn't the publicity John wanted or needed to launch himself into the private security industry.

Private security was one of the fastest growing businesses throughout the 1970s. The world's headlines were dominated by the upsurge in international terrorism. The Black September group had murdered the Israeli hostages taken at the Munich Olympics. Red Brigade anarchists had embarked on a campaign of kidnap and murder in Germany and Italy. The Italian Prime Minister, Aldo Moro, was kidnapped and then killed in cold blood. South Moluccan terrorists had seized a whole trainload of hostages in Holland and, on the UK mainland, innocents were slaughtered as the IRA planted bombs with murderous intent.

The public demanded to know what was to be done about it, as it seemed the authorities were powerless.

Then, in May 1980, there was some welcome relief. When a group of dissidents took over the Iranian Embassy in London, holding the occupants hostage, Prime Minister Margaret Thatcher ordered in Britain's elite force, the SAS. Millions were thrilled the world over to see, on prime time TV, a daring rescue that could have been a scene in a movie, where the terrorists were all killed or captured and the hostages freed.

That was more like it, crowed the public in gung-ho mood. Don't mess about any more – send in the SAS – snatch those known to be guilty wherever they may be hiding and return them to justice. In the United States, President Ronald Reagan promised a harder line against terrorism and in Britain, Margaret Thatcher resolved never to give in to terrorist demands.

The SAS, or Special Air Service, had developed from Colonel David Stirling's Long Range Desert Group which carried out dangerous behind-the-lines missions in North Africa during the Second World War. Its members who retired, as age took its toll on the high level of physical fitness required, still found their talents in demand however, mainly in the security field. Many foreign countries sought the benefit of their unique expertise. They guarded statesmen, helped defeat armed insurrections and were called in as consultants on matters affecting military intelligence. Their reputation for discretion was of the highest.

With this growth in terrorism throughout the world the security business boomed. At the lower end of the scale, people like John Miller made themselves busy guarding pop stars, offering personal protection services to industrialists, tin-pot dictators, or anyone who would employ them, with no questions asked.

The upper end of the market was controlled by people like Sir David Stirling himself and an exclusive clique of trusted ex-officers who had graduated from the SAS and various Guards regiments. They were envied by Miller and his mates. Disparagingly, they would be referred to as the 'Guards Mafia'.

The 'Guards Mafia' was not unaware of the other ranks and was quite prepared to use them in lesser tasks, or when they were not prepared to take the risk of bad publicity attaching itself to their own activities. It was with this in mind that a senior government official, who worked for a very secret intelligence department, gave serious consideration to the Biggs scandal, and what might be done about it.

Criminals escaping justice were becoming a public embarrassment, making the authorities a laughing stock. There were bank robbers living with impunity in Spain, on what had become known as the *Costa del Crime*, because the Spanish authorities refused to allow extradition proceedings. A similar case existed in Malta, where a known murderer, John Gaul, was in open residence. In the Netherlands, British paedophiles, some wanted by Scotland Yard for murder, were openly trading their filth. General Idi Amin, having conveniently converted to Islam, escaped to Saudi Arabia. And South America was home from home for hundreds of Nazi war-criminals, including the much-wanted Dr Mengele.

Another area where Britain felt most frustrated was in its battle with terrorism and its inability to bring known perpetrators to justice. In the ongoing war with the IRA it was the pre-eminent issue in Anglo-Irish relations at the beginning of the 1980s. For years, Irish judges refused to extradite known IRA bombers to Britain and, in the United States, a 'political offences' loophole was used to allow wanted IRA men there to escape trial.

The public was saying something ought to be done about this scandal and the press had taken up the cry against the government. But how could any effective action be taken in such cases without creating yet another uncomfortable diplomatic incident?

There was nothing new in covert activities for military purposes. When governments need to intervene in other countries with delicate political problems, it makes sense to use contract soldiers, or mercenaries, the advantage of such missions is that they are 'deniable' if anything goes wrong. The British, French, Americans and Israelis had all used such covert activities.

The senior official mulled over the possibility of capturing Ronnie Biggs. True, to conduct a clandestine operation against a civilian fugitive accorded sanctuary by a 'friendly' sovereign state might have its own problems. Again the protection of some IRA members by the USA came to mind. Was now the time to test the water? Biggs was now a criminal celebrity and a thorn in the side of the British Establishment. But he was also a non-political target and therefore an ideal test case. This was a job – though at arm's length, of course – for a group of trained former soldiers, expendable if necessary. It would take time to devise a workable plan and would need to be completely under cover.

The official picked up a phone and called a friend, someone who had the right connections, a former senior officer in the Coldstream Guards. The least they could do was to have a chat about it. Every option was negotiable, so long as it did not involve the government.

PART
THREE

A personal tale…

THE DRUM CLUB

When I was a youngster anyone in a soldier's uniform was a hero. I could sit for hours, listening to the veterans of two world wars talk about their exploits. This fascination with military history led me first to the army and ultimately to a career as producer and director of television documentaries.

I guess a love of adventure was in my genes. In 1902, Great Uncle Fred Stock had been one of the original pioneers in Rhodesia who, as a fourteen-year-old boy, arrived in the country in a wagon pulled by a team of oxen. My great grandfather made his fortune by pioneering the first steam laundry in London. His son, another Uncle Fred Stock had been one of the first pilots in the Royal Flying Corps before emigrating to Kenya to plant coffee. Grandfather John Edwin Lloyd King was a cavalry officer with the 17th Lancers, wounded in the First World War and later transferred to the Grenadier Guards.

My father, Richard King, was a champion horseman and looked every inch the dashing hero. During the Second World War he served in the Oxford and Buckinghamshire Light Infantry from Normandy to Berlin. In 1947 he was posted to the Trieste garrison in Italy where he met and married my mother, Mary, a war widow whose family had an equally adventurous history. The newly married captain and his wife were posted to Field Marshall Viscount Bernard Montgomery's staff in Germany, where I was born.

Later, my parents separated. Father left the army and moved to Malawi in Africa whilst my mother and I came to England where I was educated at a series of private schools in North London. When it was time to choose a career I was torn between my desire to work in the film industry or fulfilling the family tradition of joining the army. I attended an army recruits course at the Gordon Highlanders barracks in Aberdeen but a full time career in the army was looking less attractive to an ambitious teenager living through the swinging Sixties.

It was my father who solved the problem for me. He told me to get the best of both worlds by remaining a civilian and joining the new Territorial and Army Volunteer Reserve. When it came to choosing a regiment, for me it had to be the famous London Scottish, then part of the 51st Highland Volunteers. The TA had a tremendous spirit, its trained soldiers taking part in all the activities of the regular army. It also had an excellent social side where contacts and friendships would be made for life. Some of these have served me well over the years.

By the late Sixties I was working in the film industry, my knowledge of military uniforms being employed on films like *Waterloo* and *Patton* and the acclaimed British TV series *Dad's Army*. But I wanted more adventurous pursuits. In 1974 I got the idea of opening a private members' drinking club in the West End of London but was very short of cash. Then, on a visit to my father in Malawi, I met Brian Davidson, a former Rhodesian policeman who knew about my family connections with Rhodesia. Davidson explained that the guerrilla war being waged by rebel factions – one of them led by Robert Mugabe – was escalating fast. Davidson suggested he could arrange the money I needed but, in return for full financial backing, he wanted me to recruit skilled personnel for Rhodesia, which was short of pilots, electricians, radar operators and mechanics. It would have to be a clandestine operation because of sanctions against the country.

A private members' club in the Seventies was exempt from the archaic licensing laws that were then in force. By law, anyone who entered the premises to drink would have to fill out an application form for membership – an excellent way of getting basic information on prospective recruits. The Drum Club was an ideal cover. Being the owner gave me the chance to chat with the patrons, mostly ex-servicemen, finding out details of their professional and personal lives. I could then pass on any useful 'info' to an appointed case officer who would arrange for a suitable candidate to be approached. Opening the Drum Club was a first step into the shadowy world of security.

Since the club was in the heart of London's West End, it also attracted a colourful local crowd. Two of its patrons were to play major roles in my life. The first of them came crashing through the club door, having tripped at the entrance, landing heavily on a table which collapsed under his weight.

'What the hell's going on?' I asked, peering over the bar.

'Sorry mate,' replied the heap on the floor.

One look at Fred Prime was enough to convince me he was a man to befriend, not offend. The apologetic hand offered was the largest I've ever seen. The accompanying enormous laugh, a roar in fact, together with the apology and the stumbling, were something I would get used to over the next thirty years.

The club members enjoyed Fred's company. Although quite fearsome in appearance, he was good fun to be with. He had enjoyed his twelve years in the Scots Guards and the kudos of being an army boxing champion. His posting to Malaya, along with his wife, Kathleen, and two daughters, Debbie and Karen, had been an exciting experience, until tragedy struck the family. Debbie, just eighteen months old, became infected by a mosquito bite and was so seriously ill, she had to be flown back to Britain. The illness developed into encephalitis, acute inflammation of the brain, and Debbie fell into a coma which lasted until her death, twelve years later.

After that experience, the army lost its appeal and Fred found himself back on Civvie Street. At first he drifted into the private security business but found London's flourishing music clubs not only more fun but more lucrative. He worked as a minder at the concerts and rock festivals which were becoming a regular feature on the British pop scene.

The Drum Club's landlord, John Howard, also owned the adjacent property, 20 Hanway Street, so I took out a lease on the ground floor to use as a store room. Living in the top flat of number 20 was another of Fred's former comrades, John Miller, who was in the process of buying himself out of the Scots Guards. As a neighbour, Miller used the club and, like Fred, enjoyed the company of the clientele the club attracted.

The club was on the first floor of a slightly decrepit Victorian building. Two floors above the club, a call-girl named Carol entertained clients in a small flat. On summer evenings, when the club's door onto the landing was open, Fred liked watching the clients go up and, after a suitable interval, would try to spot them as they came down to see whether they looked happy or miserable.

Fred was a useful man to have around the club. When Antonio, a part-time flamenco dancer, got drunk one day he decided to show the other members his dancing abilities. For a man who was half English and half Gibraltarian and whose real name was Jim, his flamenco was not bad. However he was in no fit state to stand, let alone dance. The well-oiled Antonio got too close with his castanets to a man in the audience and kept clapping him on the head. Antonio's so-called performance came to an abrupt end when he trod on the feet of the increasingly enraged patron, who got up and punched the hapless dancer in the mouth. Unfortunately for both, the fracas had made Fred spill his beer. Both were thrown out of the Drum head first.

At the age of twenty-five I was the owner of a thriving business. So it was not long before John Miller was offering me a variety of business opportunities. John had always been fascinated with the pop music business and asked Fred Prime and me to form a company with him, called Entertainment Security.

The business started well enough. Miller had befriended an impresario named John Martin and secured a lucrative contract at the Drury Lane Theatre in London to provide security for a series of one-day musical shows known as *Sundays at the Lane*. Our company would provide off-duty soldiers as minders, pay them five pounds each, and charge the theatre fifteen pounds per man. We looked after some of the biggest names of the period, including The Supremes, Gary Glitter, The Four Seasons and Frankie Lane. It was at the Frankie Lane concert that things went bad. A mini riot developed during the support act when some boisterous teeny boppers got out of hand and the Council Safety Officer threatened to close the show. Every security man was needed to control the fans but John was missing. Initially concerns were for his safety. That is until he was discovered on the floor of the Royal Box, in a compromising position with the impresario's secretary, and that was the end of that contract.

Subsequently, Miller and I tried a variety of different ventures, including managing two rock bands, but the partnership didn't really work. I suppose I was the more serious, concerned with detail, while John had a casual approach. Although we remained friends, the business relationship ended.

In 1977, when the authorities discovered that Rhodesian Intelligence was behind the venture, the Drum Club was forced to close. But it had given me enough of a nest egg to turn my attention back to the media business and I started a production company called Piper International. I used the company to develop ideas for films and television, as well as a news agency. At first, apart from a few stories, business was pitifully slow. The shadowy security associates from the Drum Club, however, still kept in contact and began offering me new and interesting propositions. I was soon making a reasonable living from security work.

Much of this involved surveillance, a task that often needed two-way radios. In those days frequencies and even simple CB radios were controlled by the Home Office. To get round this problem, I took over a small motorbike courier and cab service in North London which already had a fully licensed radio system. The operatives, either on motorbikes or in cars, if stopped and questioned as to why they were loitering in a particular area, could claim to be couriers just waiting for a job. If checked, this would be confirmed by the licensed office. Although our success rate soared this wasn't really the work I wanted. It was the more adventurous international business with the potential of greater returns that beckoned.

Opportunities began to present themselves through my father, who had become managing director of a specialist insurance brokers for southern Africa, a subsidiary of Hogg Robinson, at that time the largest brokers in the United Kingdom. This enabled me to meet and cultivate high level contacts, many of whom were African or Middle Eastern businessmen with access to lucrative security contracts. In fact it was Hogg Robinson who was behind the creation of Control Risks Limited, a company specialising in hostage negotiation. Employing former Special Forces officers, Control Risks became a highly successful private security organisation used by Lloyds underwriters as well as many other large international companies.

By 1979, while John Miller was embarking on his publicity stunt to capture Ronald Biggs from Brazil, I was carefully carving out my own niche market in international security. I could see an opening for myself as a broker, putting clients in touch with the right people. I had good connections and was soon gaining a reputation as someone who could deliver.

However, my earlier association with Miller had not gone unnoticed by certain people. John's obsession to capture Ronnie Biggs had motivated others to hatch an audacious plot!

When the Great Train Robbery took place in August 1963, coincidentally only a few miles from my grandmother's house in Buckinghamshire, I was only thirteen years old. It was the summer holiday and I was leading my gang of chums in 'scrumping', the traditional British schoolboy pursuit of raiding apple orchards.

The train robbery was, of course, big news, and we would listen to the adults airing their views: 'What an incredible cheek robbing the Royal Mail!'…'How shocking!'…'Hurting that poor train driver, hang 'em, I say!'…'What is the world coming to, Mrs King?' people would ask my grandmother.

Little did I know that eighteen years later my path would cross that of Ronald Biggs. Although still part of a gang, this time the target wasn't English apples but the train robber himself. The link in the chain of events that brought the two of us together was John Miller, the charismatic Scotsman in search of celebrity.

TAKING SYRUP

My involvement with Ronald Biggs began, bizarrely, to the skirl of the bagpipes! It was October 31st 1980, Halloween, and more than four hundred people had gathered in the splendid Victorian drill hall of the London Scottish Regiment for the Annual Dinner. I rarely missed the event, and my guest for the evening was Fred Prime.

The occasion commemorates the day in 1914 when the London Scottish became the first Territorial regiment to see action on the Western Front. In accordance with Scottish tradition, the first course of the dinner is always haggis, an alleged 'delicacy' made from sheep's offal, chopped up with suet, onions, oatmeal and seasoning, all boiled in a bag of tripe made from the sheep's stomach lining.

With fitting ceremony for this gastronomic delight, the Pipe Major entered, cheeks flared, bagpipes blaring, playing the traditional tune 'A Man's a Man for a' That', followed by the chef carrying the haggis on a silver platter. Greatly applauded, the procession continued to the top table where the Regimental Colonel, dirk in hand, proclaimed to the diners the virtue of the dish, in the words of Robbie Burns:

> *Fair fa' your honest sonsie face*
> *Great chieftain o' the pudden race,*
> *Afore them a' ye tak' your place,*
> *Pauch, tripe or thairm,*
> *Weel are ye worthy o' a grace,*
> *As long as my airm.*

Dramatically, the Colonel plunged the ten inch blade of his dirk into the quivering mass, after which the chef took over and carved portions for everyone as a first course.

I must admit I found the taste a little too bitter for my liking, and poured whisky on it, an accepted practice in the London Scottish, though the addition of 'Scottish gravy' was frowned on by purists. Fred was looking uneasily at his plate, so I passed him some 'Scottish gravy'. Fred, however, poured the whisky down his throat and left the haggis to fend for itself.

The rest of the evening passed in a haze of reminiscence with ribald jokes shouted across the table. Then came the speeches followed by an entertainment of rousing pipes and drums. I'd been a drummer in the band for twelve years and left the table to collect my drum and play. The band was a hobby and I enjoyed playing the rousing tunes of glory that made the Scottish regiments so special. Finally, Drum Major Brian Alderson barked out orders to play the regimental march, 'Highland Laddie', and this marked the end of the formal proceedings. Gradually the gathering dispersed to one of the three bars, where the more hardy were apt to stay until the early morning, chatting with friends and consuming vast quantities of good malt whisky.

I stayed on to hear my old friend, John Spoore, personal piper to the Queen Mother, play a final set to noisy acclaim. I was just thinking of leaving myself, when a man came up to me and introduced himself as Major Bob Halford.

This kind of informal introduction is common at the London Scottish and I accepted the invitation to have a drink. Halford was fiftyish with the red cheeks and hale appearance of a farmer. He did not seem to know anyone there in the bar, nor they him, but it was clearly no accident that he had homed in on me. He seemed to know quite a lot about me, although he did not explain how he knew and, following some small talk about what a great evening it had been, asked for my telephone number, saying that an acquaintance of his was looking for someone working in the security line.

I gave him my business card, interested to know more. Halford said he had to go, however, and, finishing his drink and declining the offer of another, did just that. I then got involved with a group of army musicians and ended up grogging the night away with them. The next morning I could barely remember meeting the mysterious Major Halford.

I was reminded when there was a telephone call a week or so later from someone who identified himself as Ray Jarrett. In a well-spoken English accent, Jarrett invited me to meet him for tea, at the Park Lane Hotel, in London, to discuss some business.

Jarrett, probably in his fifties, was five foot ten and slenderly built. Conventionally dressed he looked a military type but wore no club or regimental tie. 'I work as a security consultant, currently for an American client,' he said. 'We are undertaking a research project and I think your company may be of use to us.'

Jarrett lit a cigarette and I noticed his nicotine-stained fingers. 'The group I represent,' he continued, 'are researching the feasibility of bringing fugitives, hiding in foreign countries, back home to face justice.' The whole statement was so pretentious, I was inclined to burst out laughing but thought it better not to start on the wrong foot.

'You must be joking?' I enquired courteously. The other man coolly blew out a wreath of smoke and shook his head. 'What for? And why me?'

Jarrett smiled. 'I believe you know, and have worked with, John McKillop?'

My smile faded. Where did Jarrett get the name McKillop from? It was Miller's real name but he had not used it for years.

'Big John Miller – the Scotsman?' I asked.

'Yes, you may remember about eighteen months ago he was involved in a publicity stunt to kidnap Ronnie Biggs in Brazil...?'

'Of course I do. Who doesn't? It made quite a stir.'

Jarrett took another drag on his cigarette and leaned forward. 'We need you to approach Miller, to see if he is interested in repeating the episode.'

This time I did laugh.

'Pat, I am not joking, my clients take this matter quite seriously.'

'I'm not in the kidnap game,' I told him.

'There is no need for you to be directly involved. We're not asking you to do anything illegal.' He stubbed out his cigarette and immediately lit a fresh one.

Jarrett went on to justify his argument: arresting a fugitive wanted for a crime, even more – one convicted of a crime – could not in itself be a criminal act. There might be political and diplomatic reasons why unconventional means to an end might need to be sought but they could surely be justified. This could not possibly be judged a kidnapping in either the political or legal sense. Political kidnappers demand concessions and criminal kidnappers demand ransom. In this case, neither of these options would ever be sought.

'Why should I do this? I mean is there any official backing?' I asked.

'Come now Pat, you know better than to ask that sort of direct question,' laughed Jarrett. 'Lets put it this way, we could offer some lucrative security contracts, to the right people.'

'Like me?' Jarrett nodded. He was obviously well-informed about my clandestine work in the Drum Club five years earlier when I had recruited ex-servicemen for the struggle in Rhodesia, as well as the sanctions-busting activities. He even knew the names of my current Saudi Arabian clients.

My interest was heightened. This man was clearly no joker but someone possibly associated with British Intelligence perhaps or, given his cover story, even the CIA. As of now, there was nothing to lose by going along with him.

'OK,' I shrugged, 'If the terms are acceptable I'll find Miller for you.'

Jarrett leaned forward again. 'I don't just want Miller, I want you.' There was a short pause. 'We'll pay you $5,000* in advance to act as broker with ourselves and Miller, and whoever else might be in the team. We need you to conduct a feasibility study on capturing Biggs. What do you think?' There was another pause.

'All for five thousand dollars?'

Jarrett smiled. 'You're a smart young man and there is always work in our business for people like you. Rest assured, we will see to it that within a few short weeks after, your company will receive a lucrative contract. Let's call it a damn good bonus. Agreed?'

It was now my turn to smile. What was there to say? Either Jarrett was a bullshitter, mad or genuine. The whole meeting was as intriguing as hell. Obviously I couldn't give up now.

'Do you want me to fix up a meeting with John?'

'Good God, no!' howled Jarrett. 'Miller's a loose cannon. We want to keep him at arm's length. That's why we're paying you, to act as a broker – the middle-man.'

I guessed how Jarrett must be thinking. For a deniable operation, Miller was the ideal candidate: he had all the ability as a soldier to pull this off, he was a natural buccaneer, but his weakness was his own ego. If he failed, he would be the perfect fall-guy, an obsessive who was trying to put right his mistakes of two years ago. Jarrett obviously knew more about Miller than he was letting on, which, when I finally nodded my acceptance, he confirmed by reeling off a list of John's previous brushes with the law, the army and the press.

We shook hands and I promised to get in touch with him when I'd contacted Miller. At least, I thought, it would be an adventure.

First of all I made contact with Fred Prime. Although I knew the story of the first so-called kidnap pretty well, I sat him down and got him to go through the whole caper, getting a blow by blow account. There were details lacking, of course,

---

* worth $20,000 today

since Fred could only relate the story from his own point of view and whatever Miller had told him. It was enough for me to confirm what I'd always thought: that if John had not blabbed to the press, they could actually have got away with it. The modus operandi had worked satisfactorily and, if Miller could be held in check, might be employed again, this time with more effect.

Through Fred, I arranged a meeting later that week with John Miller. I was a bit circumspect with him but there was no point in trying to keep secret the object of the mission. Indeed the prospect of being given the chance to put right the failure of two years ago obviously fired John's imagination.

Fred Prime had actually liked Ronnie Biggs and had got on very well with him. But the issue was clear cut as far as he was concerned. He had nothing against Ronnie Biggs – he would just be obeying orders: the rigours of army discipline had lodged the concept of duty, obeying orders without question, firmly in Fred's mind.

Miller's mind-set was quite different. When Ronnie's name came up in conversation it seemed as if John despised him. He appeared to condemn Biggs for having left his wife and children in the lurch, just to save himself, and for then living it up in Rio. Most of all he strongly resented the fact that it was mainly Biggs who had profited from the publicity from the kidnap stunt out of which John had hoped to make a fortune. On the one hand this facilitated Miller's escape from the Brazilian police, but on the other it robbed him of the fame he so desperately craved.

It was Ronnie who had capitalised on the event by going to the police and complaining that these men were trying to kidnap him, and it was the cops who had pulled them in on Ronnie Biggs' word! In John's view, Biggs must have known what he was doing. Ronnie had already savoured the tang of newspaper headlines following the Jack Slipper debacle and had slimily grabbed at the chance of a follow-up – and he had been right!

It was Biggs who had come out the hero, Biggs who had written a book on the subject, Biggs they'd made a film about. This thief had made a fortune out of their enterprise while they had been made to look fools, failures and publicity-grubbing vultures. So far as Miller was concerned, the aura surrounding the invincibility of Ronnie Biggs made him feel sick!

I let Miller run on, probing him on the details of the operation. What was clear was that Miller needed no motivation to have a second crack at kidnapping Ronnie. But could he be controlled?

A further two weeks elapsed before Jarrett rang again, this time to arrange a meeting for me to report back to him. It was already early December and I needed another two weeks to finalise plans, so we agreed to get together after Christmas, early in the New Year.

On Monday January 5th 1981, I went to the St Ermin's Hotel in Caxton Street, Victoria, where Jarrett was staying. I'd made a mental note that this prospective employer always chose conservative, rather old-fashioned hotels rather than the Hilton or Intercontinental where most Americans go. So who were Jarrett's American clients – were they the CIA? But what interest would the CIA have in going after Biggs? I'd learnt some time ago that sometimes it was better not to ask too many questions.

I began by explaining to Jarrett the different options. The actual mechanics of snatching Ronnie didn't strike me as a real problem for a trained team. It was the location that was difficult. Rio de Janeiro, where Biggs lived, had a population of ten million people and was not the easiest of places to get out of once the fugitive had been captured. Where could we go?

Brazil is the fifth largest country in the world, and an escape by land was out of the question since the nearest bordering countries were Argentina and Uruguay, both many kilometres from Rio. Furthermore, neither country had an extradition treaty with the United Kingdom. An escape by sea from Rio would entail sailing directly from the South Atlantic to Britain, a three to four week journey in a small yacht. Apart from the great distance, there was the possibility of being stopped by Brazilian customs or police, who were on constant alert for drug runners. This was too risky.

To escape Rio by air seemed the only option. To fly the six thousand miles directly to Britain however, would require an airliner such as a McDonald Douglas DC8 freighter, an expensive choice. Also a team flying directly into a British airport would almost certainly be arrested on arrival. Even on release they would be at the mercy of a baying press corps, who would by then know their identities. To avoid this unwanted attention would mean flying to Holland or the Republic of Ireland, where the authorities were known to be more 'relaxed'. The team could then transfer their captive to a waiting helicopter and fly to British territorial waters. There, Biggs would be lowered into a rowing boat to await the arrival of the police, which would also allow ample time for the team to disappear. But the cost of flying direct to Europe looked prohibitive.

The only remaining and feasible option was to take the fugitive to an intermediate country which had an extradition treaty with the United Kingdom. Using Miller's original idea as a template, a more detailed plan had been devised. Once Biggs had been snatched in Rio, he would be taken by private jet to Belem, a port in northern Brazil, and then transferred to a waiting yacht which would sail him to Barbados.

Belem stood on the banks of the River Para, a tributary of the mighty Amazon. Sailing time to the Atlantic was just over twenty-four hours and, although the team would not be safe until they reached international waters, it was a risk worth taking.

Total sailing time from Belem to Barbados would be six to seven days depending on the weather. Of all the Caribbean islands, Barbados was the most British. Its laws and civil service followed the British systems and most important of all it had an extradition treaty with Britain, which enabled criminals from either country to be deported on request.

The two most expensive items of equipment needed for this option were the private plane and the ocean-going yacht. The ideal choice of aircraft was a Lear Jet 125, capable of flying the three hours without having to stop at the country's capital, Brasilia, for refuelling, a process which required all passengers to disembark – not a good idea with a body bagged up inside. The ocean-going yacht would be hired directly in Antigua, though not by telex as in Miller's 1979 attempt, so the skipper could be checked out.

When I had finished elaborating the options, Jarrett poured more whisky for me. 'Excellent,' he said, 'it's all there. You've covered all the options. Well done, old man.'

'OK, thanks, but where do we go from here?'

Jarrett took a large gulp of whisky and made a decision. 'For all overall purposes it is important, in fact vital, that the subject is taken to a third country to be extradited. Barbados is ideal so that is the plan we will go with.'

Now that the plan was agreed, he wanted me to set up a meeting with Miller while Jarrett himself remained incognito. The cover story we came up with was to be that I would arrange a lunch for the two of us and with others, all posing as potential investors.

The idea that would be pitched was that these investors in the project would be looking to recoup their investment and make a profit from the extensive media sales that would be a corollary of a successful operation in the months following Biggs' extradition – having, as it were, an 'exclusive'.

I reckoned I could provide the necessary bogus investors to give Jarrett his cover. It would be a convincing scenario for John to swallow and the occasion would serve the purpose of allowing Jarrett to meet the foot-soldiers without revealing his own role of commanding officer!

* * *

A meeting was set up of all the interested parties at the Hendon Hall Hotel in north London. I booked a private room to give lunch to the two sides, John Miller, Fred Prime and myself on the one hand, Jarrett and the two bogus investors on the other.

I got John Howard, an old family friend, to assist in the ruse and he had brought along his associate, Vic Burrell, to add to the image of authenticity. I supervised the proceedings, hosting the excellent lunch, each course accompanied by appropriate wines. A party atmosphere soon began to develop. John Miller was in top form. The backers threw a few questions which he fielded admirably. Fred was laughing with Howard. Even Jarrett was smiling.

The budget for the enterprise was calculated in American dollars and had been set at $70,000 with $10,000 for contingencies*. Howard agreed, with his partner's consent, to put up half. Jarrett agreed to put up the other $35,000. Both parties would meet *pari passu* any claim on the contingency fund. The negotiations were all concluded remarkably smoothly. Of course, I'd assured Howard that there would never be any call on his supposed subscription.

A provisional date in March was set for the expedition and a $20,000 advance agreed to set the ball rolling: to recruit the rest of the team, secure the yacht, purchase all necessary stores and equipment. The operation was in green light mode. Everyone was ecstatic except me when the hotel banqueting manager handed me the bill!

There was no official code-name for the expedition but we had humorously designated it as *Taking Syrup* from the Cockney rhyming slang Fred employed, *Syrup* being Ronnie Biggs, or *Syrup of figs*.

---

* Total budget worth $320,000 today

ALL THE QUEEN'S MEN

On February 12th, I met Ray Jarrett at the Hyde Park Hotel to collect an agreed sum of $20,000 to get the show on the road. The operation, now re-christened 'Anaconda', much to Fred Prime's annoyance, was running on a time clock. The allocated start date was only two weeks away and there were a number of logistical arrangements to be considered.

Recruitment of the team was the first priority. I'd been designated the 'Quartermaster' and was to be based in London. Once the team had captured Biggs, I would fly to Barbados to prepare the way for the captive to be handed over to the authorities and then arrange for the quiet dispersal of the team from the island back to Britain. John Miller, of course, was in charge of the snatch team and Fred Prime agreed to 'babysit' Ronnie throughout the voyage from Brazil to Barbados.

John had recently been working at a club called the Venue in Victoria, where he had befriended Mark Algate, a twenty-seven-year-old from Surrey, and former soldier in the Royal Engineers. Apart from being a body-builder, Mark had qualified as a commando, and was competent in watercraft. On paper he was suitable in every way but his appearance was worrying. His arms were covered in tattoos which made him very noticeable. Mark also had a bad temper, but Miller felt he could control him. As John said, this wasn't going to be a picnic, and Algate would be useful in a tight spot.

It was Mark Algate who introduced Londoner Tony Marriage to the team: they had served together in the Royal Engineers. Although only twenty-six years old, Tony had completed several specialist courses and was a trained medic, which would be very useful if Biggs went into shock or some other emergency arose. Mark explained that Tony had been nicknamed, 'The Chameleon' for his skills in surveillance and had done extensive undercover work in Northern Ireland. When offered the chance to join our team, Tony said, 'Adventures don't come along often in one's life.' It was the kind of reasoning that appealed to both John and me.

It had been decided earlier in the planning that a male and female, posing as man and wife, would be the ideal cover when contacting Biggs in Rio, appearing less suspicious to Ronnie's friends after Miller's 1979 attempt. Finding a woman operative with the right qualifications proved very difficult. A former policewoman with the Royal Ulster Constabulary had sounded perfect for the job but, when approached, she declined the offer.

So this last piece of the jigsaw was still missing. The operation could not go forward without the right person for the covert job of contacting Biggs. With time running out, Jarrett suddenly shook me with the suggestion that I should go myself.

This was definitely not part of my plan. It seemed to me I'd done the job I was asked to do. My detailed plan had been accepted and I would follow through, making all the necessary logistical arrangements and generally administer the project. I'd never seen myself as – and it had never been agreed that I would be – part of the Rio team.

Jarrett was uncharacteristically persistent. He said he understood my reservations but the present situation would not exist if this key person, the person who had to befriend Biggs, had been identified and selected. He saw me as the obvious choice, not only because of my overall knowledge of the plan, but because I'd be there to keep an eye on John Miller.

Jarrett persuaded me that everyone would feel on safer ground if I were there and the role was absolutely essential to the abduction of Biggs. Ronnie was well known to be, as Miller himself could vouch, a slippery customer with a native cunning that always asserted itself when he smelt danger. He insisted that I had the right *persona*: I was not an outrageous extrovert like Miller and could pass myself off as a freelance journalist, an ideal cover to get near Biggs. I still had several misgivings when I accepted the logic of Jarrett's arguments. It was clear I was too far involved in the strategy of the mission to refuse. At the very least if the operation collapsed I would have a terrific story for my fledgling media agency.

The new operational team gathered for our first briefing. Each man had joined the mission for his own reasons but there were several points that needed to be discussed, including the legality of their situation.

'I don't like the word "kidnapping",' said Tony. 'None of us are, or want to be, kidnappers.'

'This isn't a kidnapping in the conventional sense,' I replied. 'It is snatching a fugitive from another country and taking him back to face justice. I have been assured we would not be breaking the law in this country.'

'You mean a citizen's arrest?' interrupted Fred Prime, 'I bet they don't see it that way if they catch us.'

'Yeah! What about Brazilian law?' asked Tony.

I told them it was important to put Brazil into proper perspective. 'Most of us see Brazil as Pele winning the soccer World Cup, or of beautiful girls parading up and down Copacabana Beach, or even saving the Amazon rain forest. Well, yes, it is those things but it's also a land that has been in the tight grip of a military dictatorship since 1964, which conducted a "dirty war" against its own citizens. There is widespread repression there.'

I tried to spell it out in full, how the police had their own death squads, unofficial vigilante units, used to perform unlawful 'necessary actions', such as political murders and the elimination of undesirables – trade unionists, drug dealers, thieves, even street children – under the guise of 'social cleansing'. In Rio, where the annual murder rate was just under three thousand, between thirty and forty children were killed every week by the police.

They listened carefully as I told them that institutional violence was a part of everyday life in Brazil. It was not a country where respect for the law was automatic. It was a place quite content to harbour fugitives, from Nazi war criminals to train robbers. It was a rogue state, one where legal issues were often decided by the contents of a wallet and, in our planning, John Miller and I had allowed about $10,000* as an emergency fund to pay off any officials if things went badly for the team. It was known as the 'PO Account' – the 'Pay Off' fund.

We then turned to the matter of equipment. As Miller's James Bond movie idea would not work twice, a new cover story was needed. We came up with the less dramatic tale of being a documentary film crew, shooting oil rigs off Brazil's northern coast. To make it more realistic, John hired some professional film equipment from London's West End.

Then came the question of how to carry a man five foot eleven inches tall and weighing about 170 pounds. An army tent bag, known as a marquee valise, was the answer, and Fred was tasked with obtaining one from an old army contact.

In the meantime, I got busy printing letterheads, as well as a few T-shirts, bearing the name of a bogus film operation called *Project 90 Film & Video Company*. John had also asked me to create an official-looking letter which could have been issued by the Brazilian Embassy in London, which he thought might come in useful in Rio. Using a razor blade, I carefully cut the Brazilian national emblem out of a guide book and pasted it at the top of a letter which had been written in Portuguese for me by a student.

* worth $40,000 today

It is the request of the Second Secretary of the Brazilian Embassy in London that should the bearer of this letter ask for assistance, it is to be granted, whenever possible.

> *By order and request,*
> *Captain Garcia,*
> *Military Attaché, London.*

I then took the sample document to be colour copied at the Rank Xerox shop in Holborn, the only place in London at the time that had a colour machine. The machine messed up the copy on the first run, leaving the document with a yellow tint but, since it looked just like parchment, I took it, much to the amazement of the shop assistant.

The next day I booked tickets for myself and John Miller to go to Antigua, where we were to charter a suitable yacht. We flew out of London's Heathrow Airport on February 19th, arriving ten hours later at English Harbour.

Taking a taxi from the airport, we went straight to Nicholson's, the island's largest charter company. As the taxi reached the top of the hill overlooking English Harbour's world famous bay, we gazed down to see it crowded with millionaire's yachts. 'Thank God for that,' commented Miller.

But it was a different story at Nicholson's, who didn't know of any available yachts to charter at such short notice, although they would continue to search for one. Feeling a bit disheartened, we registered at the luxurious Admiral's Inn. Miller headed for the bar while I went to my room for a bath.

About half an hour later there was a frantic knocking on the door. It was John Miller.

'What's up?'

'Pat, you're not going to believe this!' he began ominously.

'Oh, no! Now what?'

'I've just seen Steve Adamson sitting in the bar.'

'Who's Steve Adamson?'

Adamson turned out to be the captain of the *Ocean Scorpio*, the yacht John had hired in 1979. That was bad news but worse was to discover the hire charges had never been paid. John Miller had left the island owing $2,300 – just an oversight, Miller claimed airily.

I was furious. We would have to pay the money owing or our names would be mud round the island and we'd never be able to charter a craft.

It was decided the best thing to do was for me to go and talk to Adamson and bring him back to the room to meet Miller in private. Expecting this was some kind of gag, Adamson agreed and was amazed to find Miller really there. When the bedroom door opened and the Scotsman appeared, the captain took a step back.

'Christ! I never thought I would see you again,' he said.

'Steve, come in for a drink,' replied Miller, heartily. 'We came here specially to find you.'

In no time at all, the silver-tongued Miller was already laughing the matter off, seeking to persuade the angry captain that the non-payment for the hire had just been an oversight, while I – with gritted teeth – had no option but to back him up. Adamson believed we were working for the British government and, rather than compromise the mission and to secure his silence, we agreed to pay the $2,300 still owed by Miller when we returned to Antigua the following week.

Adamson fell for it and even offered to help. In spite of his own experience, he recommended us to a young Scottish captain, Thorfinn Maciver. The endorsement proved invaluable. The Caribbean yachting community had been the victims not only of piracy on the high seas, which was rife at that time, but also of having their boats confiscated because of craft being used by drug runners who had chartered them. There was a real feeling of paranoia on the island and unsolicited offers were frequently turned down by cautious owners – or even by their agents, who had also suffered.

So at a time when references were normally being

demanded and double-checked, testimony from a fellow captain like Adamson was enough to convince Maciver who, in turn, introduced us to a Texas millionaire, Bob Sabinske, owner of the fifty-nine foot sloop *Nowcani II*. A fee of $16,000 was agreed for the charter and I handed over $5,500 as a deposit.

The immediate business done, John and I flew back to London via New York, arriving home February 22nd. The next day we went to JD Potter at 145 The Minories, in the City of London, to collect Admiralty charts and the other navigational handbooks needed for South America and the West Indies.

That evening I met Jarrett again at the Park Lane Hotel, where the balance of the money required was handed over in cash. This posed something of a previously unforeseen difficulty however, as part of the cash consisted of £15,000 in sterling. It is true I had originally asked for some sterling before realising we would be dealing entirely in US dollars, the favoured currency in Brazil and the Caribbean.

I was wondering how best to change the money from one currency to the other at such short notice – not an easy thing to do at the time – when Miller came to the rescue. Big John was engaged to Sarah Hannam whose father was a merchant banker in the City. He, when asked if he could change £15,000 into American dollars, agreed to help. The next day I went with Tony Marriage to Leopold Joseph, merchant bankers in Gresham Street, London, and collected $33,000 cash in exchange for our British pounds.

Each of the team received a down payment of $2,000 to cover their immediate expenses before leaving Britain, and would receive a further $3,000 on their return. None of them was in it just for the cash, most believed their participation would lead to well-paid security work in the future. All of them, apart from John Miller, who had his own obsession with Biggs, believed there was official, if un-attributable, backing to the operation.

At last everything was in place and we were running right on schedule. As the members of the team assembled to depart London for the West Indies, it amused me to think that on paper we probably looked an underpaid and motley crew. However, each had received British infantry training, much of it in crowd control and, in particular, how to set up and operate snatch squads, used to take ringleaders out of riots. So everybody knew his job and that training would prove invaluable in the coming weeks.

It was Friday 27th February 1981. The game was on.

COPACABANA

The five members of the team boarded our TWA flight from London to New York City, arriving in high spirits. We were not the kind of people who would pass up a night in Manhattan and were soon partying at various clubs downtown.

The next day we flew to Antigua's international airport where we were met by Thorfinn Maciver, the young Scottish captain, and his crewman, a pleasant eighteen-year-old from North Carolina, named Greg Nelson. When we arrived at English Harbour the three members of the team who hadn't previously seen the elegant *Nowcani II* voiced their approval. Luggage was loaded and the film equipment stowed safely below deck.

Since the sun was still shining we decided to have a swim in the bay. Everybody laughed when Fred Prime, filled with sudden exuberance, pushed Mark Algate into the water. Unfortunately Mark landed on a large jellyfish which promptly stung him on the back and consigned him to twenty-four hours of considerable pain. The operation had had its first casualty.

Mark's wound, however, had not prevented us descending on the Admiral's Inn that night. We met Steve Adamson and his wife, Jane, and I paid off Millers' debt of $2,300 as promised. The hangovers from the previous night in New York were forgotten as we partied, yet again, until the early hours of the morning.

Fortunately we had until lunch-time to sleep off the effects of the previous night. It was Sunday March 1st, the trip to Barbados would take just under three days and Thorfinn had estimated that the onward journey to Belem would take a further nine days.

It was late afternoon when the *Nowcani II* steered out of the narrow entrance to English Harbour and made for the open sea. Neither John nor I were good sailors and preferred to stay up on deck as much as possible, hoping before long to find our sea legs.

Fred, on the other hand, had sailed the ocean as a merchant seaman before joining the army. 'I've travelled the seven seas, mate!' he boasted.

His experience did not stop him turning green however, as the yacht met the open seas, which were distinctly choppy. He promptly threw up over the rail, and was instantly dubbed 'Barnacle Bill' by the rest of the crew.

The first night at sea was very rough but the following morning, as we passed the island of Martinique, the water was relatively calm. It was our first full day at sea and, having only just come from the British winter, we appreciated the tropical heat. Even though there was cloud cover, the sun could certainly be felt, so we played safe by applying a sun-block lotion. Barnacle Bill promptly sneered at us for being cissies.

'Don't want that greasy muck on me,' chortled Fred derisively. Next day the only pink whale in the Western hemisphere could be seen glowing in the Caribbean. Fred had got himself badly sunburnt.

Thorfinn, the ship's captain, seemed content. He was playing with the new satellite navigation equipment that had been bought out of the charter fee. The busiest person on board was the young American crewman, Greg Nelson, who always seemed to be hauling on one rope or slacking another. The ship's cook was Veronica Campanile, a Scot of Italian descent, who unfortunately had a series of sores on her legs and was promptly dubbed 'Scabby' by Mark Algate. Veronica was aware of the men's sniggering and took an instant dislike to all of us. In fact, as far as we were concerned, it was not her legs but her appalling cooking ability that offended us. On the first night out, when all of us were feeling queasy due to the rough seas and the boat's rolling motion, she had served up a bowl of greasy moussaka which not even Fred could face. Those who had risked it had lost no time in vomiting it up again.

During the voyage John and I rehearsed the plans with the rest of the team, quietly so the crew could not overhear us. The plan was for me to leave the vessel in Barbados together with Tony Marriage, who would be my back-up man. The two of us would fly Eastern Airlines to Miami, catching the PAN-AM flight next day to Rio, find and then set up Biggs, for which task we had a maximum of twelve days. The *Nowcani II* would delay sailing from Barbados in order to synchronise the two schedules and Friday March 13th was now set as Miller's target day for reaching Belem.

On the third day the *Nowcani II* sailed into Bridgetown harbour, the first leg of the journey. Fred was still recovering from his sunburn and Mark from his jellyfish sting, although the wound was not visible through his tattoos. Both bravely declared themselves fit for a night's carousing in the bars of Bridgetown. Tony and I waved our fellow conspirators goodbye and headed for the local airport. Everyone seemed relaxed but we were all aware of the unavoidable fact that the clock was ticking now and countdown had begun.

March 5th 1981 was a day off for Tony and me as the flight to Rio was not until 11.30 that night. We spent the day going out to Florida's Disney World and marvelled at the seemingly real-life talking automatons, enjoyed a canoe trip through the swamplands with hostile Red Indians and equally aggressive crocodiles in our wake, all the products of Disney's ingeniously inventive special effects team.

Our favourite ride, however, was the ironically named, to us at least, *Pirates of the Caribbean*. Again we were passengers in a boat gliding silently under a canopy of stars, passing by the harbours where pirates had landed and were sacking the town, carrying off whatever they could find – and a few protesting maidens too. It was all great fun.

In Barbados the rest of the gang were also enjoying themselves, drinking both the day and the night away, laughing hugely. John Miller was always the joker, the clown, and the affable Fred was usually the butt. The England cricket team were on a tour, visiting Barbados, and Miller with his considerable charm had managed to home in on the party, inviting two England players, Graham Gooch and Geoff Miller, back to the yacht for yet more drinks.

The following day Tony and I arrived in Rio, moving into the Luxor Hotel at Copacabana and immediately started work, trying to trace Biggs' whereabouts. Miller had suggested that I should look first for a man named Clive Wilson, an Englishman living in Rio who worked as a tourist travel guide and general fixer, arranging deep sea fishing charters, organising tours and so on. Among the sights of Rio he included one Ronnie Biggs and was always ready to take a party along to meet the infamous great train robber, hear his story, pose alongside him for photographs. The deal was that they split 50/50 on whatever Wilson charged. Biggs disliked him strongly but played along whenever he was short of a few bucks, which was often.

That same evening I managed to track down Wilson and rang him on the pretext of wanting to do some deep sea fishing: we arranged to meet the next day. At the same time plans were made for Tony to move to another hotel. It was important that when I became known to Biggs, I should appear to be entirely alone in the city. This also allowed Tony Marriage to operate as a free agent, possibly carrying out some surveillance work.

We took a stroll down town and found the atmosphere

considerably less salubrious. There were bars on every corner and lots of chemist shops which, judging by the traffic in and out of them, probably sold amphetamines over the counter, while stall-holders in the street markets were openly dealing crack. We saw drunken Western men stagger into garishly lit discotheques with Brazilian whores. The scent of marijuana seemed to waft everywhere. We returned early, and with some relief, to our hotel.

So this was Rio.

One thing I rated as essential was that communications should always be good. I had to be able to make and receive long-distance telephone calls, especially from or to Jarrett. In 1981 there were no mobile phones or fax machines in Rio and the switchboard was anything but digital. The operator had physically to link the individual line to the switchboard which, for overseas calls, could be a long task. I gave each of the three women working on the hotel switchboard $100, worth about four weeks' wages to them, which meant I never had the slightest problem with the telephone system.

The meeting with Wilson was to be at a popular watering hole for expatriates called Lord Jim on Ipanema Beach. I was using the alias Patrick Richards, wildlife photographer. This was not entirely untrue since I'd always been a keen photographer, particularly of animals, in the savannahs of Africa where my father lived and many of my pictures had been sold by a press agency.

I used the story that I was waiting in Rio for my wife to join me. I'd been on a photographic safari in South Africa and had flown in from Cape Town en route to Los Angeles to see my publisher. This gave Wilson the impression that I had plenty of money and was eager to spend some of it enjoying myself before the wife arrived.

There was nothing more that could be done on that day. The *Nowcani II* should by now have departed Bridgetown and be on course for Belem. It was, and John was engaged in his usual horseplay with the others, who were performing their own version of *Pirates of the Caribbean* with Miller adopting the role of Captain Hook.

So far the operation had run as smoothly as a well-oiled machine and both John and I, from our different perspectives, were confident of a successful conclusion to the adventure.

MIND GAMES

Saturday March 7th marked the first step, on Ronnie Biggs' home turf, towards his abduction. The meeting with Wilson was not until the late evening and so we decided to make a general reconnaissance.

Stepping out of the hotel, we thought that the location was an ideal one. Copacabana's multi-coloured mosaic promenade was a mile long and incredibly wide: the discipline of a few brisk walks up and down were good exercise and kept us both in necessary trim. It was a discipline we decided to keep up when Tony changed hotels, meeting at 9 a.m. on the dot by the old wooden drinks stand situated just a hundred yards from the Luxor.

Tony christened the drinks hut *Tobruk*, after the Second World War battle. His father had served with the British 8th Army, fighting through North Africa and Italy, and Tony had grown up knowing the names of all the famous battles. During our time in Rio, he nicknamed all of Copacabana's landmarks – *El Alamein, Salerno, Anzio* and so on.

On the first morning, although we were both still suffering from jet lag, we were out on the beach by 7 a.m., marvelling that even at that hour the sands were thronged with football crazy kids practising Brazil's national game. By the time it was nine o'clock, there were hundreds of beautiful girls, all with magnificent bodies, their skins a golden sheen, displayed to the full by mini-bikinis. They, in turn, brought out the men to watch them and, before long, the beach was crowded.

Tony and I ogled along with the other men for a while but then discipline set in. It was time to look for Biggs, just in case Wilson was not forthcoming that evening.

When the previous attempt by Miller had been made, in 1979, Biggs was living at Sepitiba, a run-down beach town about forty miles out of Rio, and so, hiring a Volkswagen Beetle, we drove out there. It was not difficult to find the house – we had been given the address – and we pulled up not far away, parked, and kept watch for a while.

It was uncomfortable in the car with the sun high in the sky and there was no air-conditioning unit: we sweated buckets. There was hardly anyone around and the house looked empty, so we took the risk of leaving the car and moved closer. Through the un-curtained windows we could see no sign of occupancy.

I decided not to quiz the immediate neighbours for fear of unnecessarily arousing suspicion but, since we desperately needed a drink anyway, we headed for the nearest café, just a block away. Sitting outside, I ordered for the two of us, to practise my all-but non-existent Portuguese.

'Dos guarana, por favor.'

It worked. We had tried *guarana*, a unique drink made from berries grown in Amazonia, on our first day and found it wonderfully refreshing. The café was practically deserted and, emboldened by my first stab at the language, I beckoned the proprietor across and tried to hold a conversation with him. I spoke Italian and, overlaying this with a Spanish accent, accompanied by much flamboyant arm gesturing, seemed to make myself understood. Certainly 'Ronee Beegs' was known to the proprietor and, by their nodding, to a couple of customers, but enquiries as to where we might find him produced only much shaking of heads and shrugging of shoulders. Clearly he had left Sepitiba and no one knew where he had gone.

Feeling dejected, we returned to Rio. I took my turn at driving and Tony fell asleep, both of us were still tired. My thoughts turned on how best to steer Clive Wilson. It would not be easy because I didn't want to mention Biggs by name to him, in case he warned Ronnie that someone had come looking for him. The hope was that Wilson would try to cash in on his acquaintance with the train robber.

As we entered the Rio de Janeiro city boundary Tony suddenly woke and sat bolt upright. 'I wonder where the bloomin' hell Ronnie is?' he said, scratching his head.

'Christ, you must have been dreaming about him,' I replied.

Later that night, we took a taxi to the Lord Jim in Ipanema, a pub decorated in the style of an old English tavern. I recognised the man standing at the bar from the description Miller had given me – 'Like an insurance clerk!' He was in his thirties, about five foot eleven and, when I introduced myself, replied with a middle-class accent.

Tony Marriage was passed off as someone I'd met on the plane, who had spent the day with me just for company. It was the only time that Wilson ever saw Tony.

I invited my 'guests' to have dinner and spent plenty of money on drink to help loosen Wilson's tongue. The conversation turned mostly to deep-sea fishing and how eager I was to hire a boat. I also wanted to see all the sights of Rio, of course, and managed to slip the name of Biggs into the conversation.

Wilson did not seem to want to be drawn on the topic, although he admitted to knowing Ronnie who, he thought, was still living out at Sepitiba. Tony and I exchanged glances for a fleeting moment; it seemed that Wilson did not know very much after all. I decided to persevere, however, and let Ronnie's name crop up once more as we casually chatted, but did not push it: Wilson had registered the intent of a rich photographer who would clearly pay well for an introduction. If Wilson genuinely did not know where Ronnie was living, he would soon find out. I invited him to have lunch the next day.

Guessing that lunch with Wilson was likely to be another liquid affair, I lined my stomach with a couple of pints of milk before leaving the hotel. The Meridien Hotel bar was clearly a popular meeting-place for European expatriates. Wilson introduced me to one of them, named Oscar, a Czech who was a dealer in emeralds – and a crook if ever I saw one. It was strange how all the Teutonic looking people over sixty living in Brazil, that I met, claimed to be Czechs or Poles, never Germans and most certainly not Nazi war criminals. Oscar was holding court at a table near the bar, obviously a regular one, where he was presumably negotiating dubious precious gem deals.

The local colour was fascinating but I wasn't there for that and Wilson seemed determined not to talk about Biggs. I was beginning to feel I was chasing a lame duck but yet, at the same time, was sure that Wilson did know something. So I resorted to the one remedy that never failed – money. Even though we had not yet set a date for the hire of the fishing boat, I handed over $200 as a deposit, to give the impression I was in earnest. Wilson's eyes lit up and he accepted the money with delight, inviting me to be his guest next day, lunching al fresco at Copacabana Beach.

Arriving next day at the appointed place, Wilson and I arranged our chairs so that we had a good view of the gorgeous girls stretching their limbs as they played volley ball. My true thoughts, though, ran in completely another direction – finding Biggs. Once more I slipped the name into the conversation and this time was rewarded with an explanation, which at least made sense, of his relationship with the train robber.

Curiously, the tale Wilson told was of Biggs' previous abduction. I knew the story backwards, of course, but it sounded very different coming from another angle. Biggs, it seemed, had thought that Miller and company were mercenaries engaged by Scotland Yard, and believed they had enlisted Wilson's support – which naturally enough he vehemently denied, though I knew it was not true anyway. I nodded in sympathy as Wilson explained that he had been held in suspicion by Biggs and his cronies ever since, at the same time thinking, 'What now? I've wasted two whole days with this bonzo!'

Downing the fourth gin and tonic Wilson had forced on me, I was ready to give up and start some other line of enquiry – though God knows what – when Wilson, as if to prove his credentials, pointed to a huge man, about six foot four, who was lumbering in our general direction.

'That's Armin,' he said, 'the Kraut who's Biggs' bodyguard. He might be able to fix up a meeting for you.'

'Good, good, call him over,' I said – perhaps over-enthusiastically, I thought later.

Wilson did so and introduced me as Patrick Richards, the name I was using, and then took Armin aside for a whispered chat. I couldn't hear them but the body language spelled out the message with clarity. Wilson was saying that he had a rich man in tow who would pay good money for an interview with Ronnie. He brought Armin back to the table. I noticed the German – at least this one admitted that he was German – had a kind of bodged skin graft on his right arm, and I reckoned there was the design of a swastika under the skin.

'Armin might be able to help us,' Wilson said, patting the Kraut on the back as if they were the best of mates. Armin obviously had no great love for Wilson.

'Ronnie's having a party for a few friends tonight,' he said in his heavy accent, 'at the Churrascaria, a restaurant near where he lives at Botafogo. Come round and ask him yourself, he won't mind.'

'Is that OK?' Wilson asked anxiously. 'Can you make it tonight?'

Could I make it? My head was whirling. 'I think so, I don't see why not – I'm on holiday.'

Armin nodded – not unfriendly: not to me anyway. Once again the power of money must have succeeded. I had no idea what Wilson had said or what this might cost me, but it would be worth it. Ronnie must be hard up and Armin knew he would accept any offer.

As Armin drifted away, my only thought was to escape from Wilson now and get back to let Tony know what was happening. But Wilson was not having it: he wanted to take me to a sauna – to sober up, he said. I liked that idea, as I wanted to have my wits about me that night. So I tolerated Wilson's company for another deadly hour and then managed to get away.

I discussed the turn of events with Tony as soon as I got back. The arrangement was for me to meet Clive at the Meridien at eight o'clock and then go on from there to the Churrascaria. Tony suggested that the best plan would be for him to get there fifteen minutes before, stay out of sight and then take a taxi, or walk as the case may be, to follow us to the restaurant, where he would wait patiently outside for a signal from me.

If the opportunity arose, he would tail Biggs – who did not know him – back to wherever he lived. We devised a simple signalling device. If I took a handkerchief from my pocket and made a play of blowing my nose, that meant Tony should stand by to follow Ronnie. If I did nothing, hopefully because I'd got the information we wanted, Tony would return to the hotel and wait to be contacted.

By the time Wilson and I arrived at the restaurant, Ronnie was already eating and drinking, holding court at a large table that held about a dozen people but still had a couple of empty places. Biggs was unmistakeable, I recognised him easily from his photographs. Wilson introduced me while trying to greet Ronnie as an old friend. Biggs just nodded coolly, dismissively.

The two of us sat down. Nobody seemed to pay us much attention. On the basis that everything comes to he who waits, I decided to do just that, looking around the restaurant and savouring the experience: eating at a Churrascaria is like nothing else. The tables are laid out with large bowls of different salads and fried potatoes. The waiters walk around the eating area with long swords on which are impaled large chunks of meat: different cuts of beef, lamb, pork and spiced sausages; whatever the customer desires.

It was a noisy occasion with much laughter and shouting. I

had no idea who all the people were but they were obviously Ronnie's friends and he was very much the centre of attention. He looked tanned and fit and seemed to have a word for everyone except me and Clive Wilson. I was puzzling over how best to approach Biggs – should I just shout above the others? At that moment Ronnie's gaze suddenly fixed on me and I called out, instantly feeling a complete prat for the banality: 'Hi, Ronnie, I'm from London, you know!'

Biggs replied and then immediately looked away. I hadn't heard a word he had said but there was no hint of hostility. I was pleased to see that Wilson took advantage of the moment, leaving his seat to go right up to Ronnie. I couldn't hear every word but could easily put together the sequence.

'That's a bloke called Patrick Richards and he wants some pics with you.'

'Does he know the fee?'

''Course, he's with me, Ronnie.'

'That's what I mean.'

For the first time he looked directly and meaningfully at me.

'How about tomorrow morning, eleven o'clock, pool at the Copacabana Palace?' he called out above the hubbub: 'That suit you, mate?'

'Yup, that's fine,' I replied, giving Ronnie the thumbs up and smiling like the creeps who hung around him. Anything suited me and if I looked stupid, a sucker with money to burn, that was just fine: it was how I wanted Ronnie to think of me.

As I looked away I spotted Armin Heim looking at me from across the table. The big man was clutching the same airline bag he had earlier. He had heard the exchange with Biggs and made a point of coming over to me, as if to let me know he was watching.

'I am a photographer too,' he said, opening his bag to show me. Inside was a Nikon camera and some ancillary equipment. There was also a revolver nestling there, certainly not hidden, maybe deliberately on display. I felt a brief twinge of alarm but what he took out was the camera, with which he proceeded to take photographs of me – obviously mug shots.

'I also look after Ronnie,' Armin stated. Was it a warning?

What a prick! I thought.

The time of the meeting had been set and there was little point in staying around much longer. I'd had plenty to eat and more than enough to drink, and wanted to be on the top of my game tomorrow. Everyone there would be too drunk to notice me slip away, including Wilson, and I did not want to leave with Wilson for fear of being bracketed with him, out of dislike or suspicion.

I stood for a moment outside the entrance, in particular to let the waiting Tony know I was leaving: I made no signal. Indeed, Tony arrived back at the Luxor just ahead of me.

We enjoyed a nightcap in the room as I briefed him on the events of the evening. Tony was ecstatic.

'We've cracked it,' he said, 'in three days – it's a mind-game. A bloody mind-game.'

Tony would have liked to go on, drinking to our success, but I was, by now, mentally and physically exhausted. I lay back on the bed and almost immediately fell asleep, my last thoughts being that it was too early for euphoria. As my comrades at the London Scottish might have commented, quoting the old proverb: 'There's many a slip twixt the cup and the lip…'

ROOM WITH A VIEW

It was the morning of Monday March 9th. The *Nowcani II* was scheduled to arrive in Belem late on the coming Friday, in just five days' time. There was still work to do and Tony and I were in great spirits when, after a breakfast of papaya, melon, pineapple and bananas, we started on our morning constitutional. The fruit in Brazil is terrific.

We went over our campaign plan for the day. Plainly, top of the agenda was for me to try to get on the right side of Biggs so that we could lure him to wherever the snatch would be made. We decided Tony would be outside the Copacabana Palace before me and, when the meeting broke up, continue to tail Biggs, snapping him from a safe distance with his telephoto lens.

I arrived dead on time, and Ronnie Biggs very soon after, for the eleven o'clock appointment. We sat by the poolside and I ordered drinks. Biggs wasted no time in asking for the $200* fee to be paid. I made a big show of peeling off ten twenty-dollar bills from a thick wad – clearly taken note of by Ronnie, as I'd intended.

Biggs asked me if I'd been commissioned to write the article, so I told him I was a freelance who just happened to be in Rio, had heard Ronnie Biggs was somewhere about and wanted a story with a few pictures to sell to the South African Argus group of newspapers and magazines.

Years later Biggs claimed in his book that he was suspicious

* worth $800 today

because the man who duped him had not carried a notebook like most journalists. That was exactly the reason why I pitched the idea as a photos-with-words article, so there wouldn't be any need to take notes, in case Biggs asked for a copy, which would have given him a sample of my handwriting. I was the wary one. Biggs had not been suspicious at all, certainly not once he had pocketed the two hundred bucks.

He prattled on about the Great Train Robbery, his various escapes and his time in Rio. They were well-practised lines which he'd used many times. He posed comfortably for the camera and was quite laid-back when I took a couple of shots of the two of us together, using the self-timer. He was on his third beer when he suddenly looked at his watch and announced that he would have to leave soon for another appointment.

It took me by surprise. I'd hoped for a long boozing session to give me a chance to set the trap. Now I had to think quickly on my feet.

'That's a pity, Ronnie. Let's finish tomorrow over lunch. It's on me.'

'Well, I'm not sure if...' he started to say.

'Of course I was expecting to pay more,' I quickly butted in.

Biggs looked at me, calculating. You could read his mind. What's in it for me, he was asking himself, apart from a good lunch?

'I can give you another $150. I realise you've got to make a living. Are you on?'

Ronnie was on. My assessment had been correct.

'All right, mate,' said Ronnie. 'Same time, same place?'

'Fine by me. I'll meet you here tomorrow, about the same time.'

We shook hands on it. I walked Ronnie out to the steps, to give a signal to Tony that the target was leaving and to follow him. Before Tony got the chance, however, Biggs jumped into a taxi and took off. We were left wrong-footed.

But it didn't really matter, now that I had a meeting the next day. There was time enough. Five days before the *Nowcani II* arrived.

The following day it was decided that Tony should change hotels, we didn't want to risk being seen staying together by any of Ronnie's friends. Tony found a room at the Gloria Hotel near Santos Dumont Airport and arranged to move in after breakfast.

It was also time to telephone Jarrett, to brief him for the first time since I had left London. I reported that contact had been made. Biggs was friendly and unsuspicious. There were still four days to go before the *Nowcani II* arrived at Belem and Jarrett seemed to be reasonably pleased. He was not one to offer congratulations – certainly not before the event – but he did express satisfaction that all so far was proceeding according to plan.

The object of that day's exercise was the same as the previous day. I felt I was getting close to our man and was sure that before long Ronnie would open up. If this thinking was still premature, Tony would be on hand to keep watch and – on my signal – follow Biggs to where he was staying, at the same time making a thorough recce of the area.

It struck me while talking to Tony how his appearance was changing. Each day he was beginning to look more like a local, partly due to his Italian ancestry on his mother's side. His handsome face already had a healthy sun tan. The curly brown hair, cut off jeans and faded T-shirt meant he blended easily with the local population. It was amazing! I now knew why he had been nicknamed 'The Chameleon'!

Ronnie was on time again for the second meeting at the Copacabana Hotel. It suited our purposes that he seemed to be punctual: it could be important. Clive Wilson had suggested he was unreliable, always late. That could prove a difficulty, if Ronnie fell in with what we had in mind.

He greeted me and we had a beer, chatted for a bit, and then

Ronnie suggested lunch.

'Fine by me,' I said.

'Where would you like to go?'

'You tell me, you're the local boy.'

Biggs laughed. 'That's right, from the Elephant and Castle.'

I asked him to take us to some place that was typically Brazilian. I was only there for another week or so, I told him, and wanted to absorb as much local colour as possible. The words 'local colour' made Ronnie smile.

'We'll see you get that. Listen, I know a good little place not far from here. It's one of my favourites. Do you mind walking?'

I didn't mind walking at all. It might give us a clue just how close he lived to here, and it would also give Tony an opportunity to follow us.

The restaurant specialised in *Bahian* food, which had its origins in the slave trade. The national dish, apparently, was something called *feijoada*, a mixture of rice, black beans and sausage, which was certainly very tasty. Biggs chose a strong local wine to go with it and we polished off two bottles of it in two hours, though I got less than a quarter, which suited me fine. Drink obviously loosened Biggs' tongue.

In spite of living off the high hog in Rio, and even though it was some fifteen years since he'd left England, it was clear that Ronnie was still homesick. He was a Londoner at heart and enjoyed nothing more than talking to a fellow Londoner. He was an amazing storyteller, genuinely making me laugh as he related some of his criminal exploits, not just about his part in the robbery but before then, when his greatest claim to fame was breaking into chemists' shops at night, even joking that his poor petrified middle-class wife acted as look-out.

He also made me laugh with a story about Leatherslade Farm: when they were counting out the proceeds of the train robbery, Bruce Reynolds ordered him to set light to £50,000 worth of ten shilling notes as they would be too bulky to carry.

'Burning money went against the grain – hardest fucking thing I've ever had to do, mate,' he mock wept.

Ronnie Biggs really was a charismatic character – I began to see why Fred had taken a shine to him. I knew I had to watch my drinking to stay in control, the day was still young, so I ordered a *cafezhino*, a strong black Brazilian coffee, while Ronnie finished off the bottle.

Suddenly he stood up. 'Come on,' he said, 'let's go back to my apartment and have a couple of beers.'

My stomach churned at the thought of more booze but I eagerly consented to the suggestion: this was exactly what the exercise was all about. At the same time, I was determined to stay wary and, if possible, avoid too much alcohol. What with the beers and wine consumed so far, we both staggered out of the restaurant.

Ronnie called a cab and we piled in. I'd momentarily forgotten about Tony, faithfully on watch, but it didn't matter now: we were bound for the beast's lair. Ronnie gave the cabbie orders and then said:

'Christ, I'd forgotten where we were. My pad's only just round the corner!'

We were still laughing as we tumbled out of the cab a few minutes later. I recognised the location – we'd reconnoitred the area thoroughly: this was Botafogo Beach, a neighbourhood not far from central Copacabana.

Ronnie's apartment was high up in the tallest apartment block in Botafogo. I was amazed that Ronnie could afford to live in such luxury. How did he do it? The money from the robbery must be long gone. True, there had been all that publicity and no doubt he cashed in on that, but that must have faded by now. Ronnie was reduced to cadging a few hundred dollars – usually a lot less probably – while he entertained with his song-and-dance routine about the robbery.

The views from the living room windows were stunning. Just below was a small and very pretty marina, while there was a panoramic view of the bay, dotted with dozens of yachts. The two great landmarks of Rio were both clearly visible, to one side *Pao de Açúcar*, the Sugar Loaf Mountain, to the other the giant statue of Christ the Redeemer overlooking the city.

In the course of the conversation, it turned out that the lease of the apartment was owned by a rich young American, a friend of Ronnie's, who had returned to the States temporarily, allowing Ronnie to take over the place while he was away. It was a rash decision since it also meant Ronnie paying the rent, which he didn't do, not for long anyway. As I found out later, after three months he was out of there.

I needed to get some pictures before we were too plastered – me to aim the camera and Ronnie to pose. It was also a good opportunity to photograph the apartment, just in case. Tony Marriage could look after the outside of the building. While I was snapping the views from different angles, Ronnie suddenly shouted, 'Hang on!'

He rushed out of the room and returned almost immediately, his face beaming.

'Nobody's done this one before,' he said, holding up a wonderful poster for the film *Robbery*, made in 1967 by screen hard-man Stanley Baker, of *Zulu* fame. The film was based on the Great Train Robbery and Biggs posing against the poster would make a terrific shot. Ronnie obligingly held up the poster, laughing and pointing to the strapline across the title: *Who says crime doesn't pay? £3 million says it does!*

'How about that?' he laughed. Cocky bugger, I thought, you're just taking the piss out of the country.

Then, using the self-timer, I took a picture of us together on the luxurious sofa, with me holding up a copy of the *Sun* newspaper, making sure the front page was exposed to the lens, to date the picture from the newspaper headline.

That particular edition of the *Sun* had a feature article in it about Biggs and his forthcoming book *My Own Story*, written for him by David Levy, who was to figure more prominently in Ronnie's own story at a later date.

I took that photograph because if plans went wrong and we were picked up by the police, we could argue that the kidnap attempt was a publicity stunt for the book, made with Biggs' full approval – hence the picture, which showed Ronnie and me discussing the article in the *Sun*, promoting the book.

It was necessary for the team to have a cover story and we'd discussed the possibilities in detail before leaving London. Each stage of the operation presented new problems with John Miller and Fred Prime being most at risk. Although they had not been deported from Brazil, they were known by the police through their previous stunt. If arrested in Rio, the authorities would probably deport them for causing an affray. However, if arrested in Belem, that would be more tricky. They would have to bluff their way out by claiming it was a publicity stunt for Ronnie's book. None of us believed the Brazilians would jail five Britons on the word of a convicted train robber: they would probably prefer to get rid of the problem by simply deporting the team.

Now that Ronnie was a free man, through a legal technicality, he had lost a good deal of the glamour attached to being a wanted man, forever on the run, using his cunning to outwit the authorities. He was free but a prisoner in Rio, still bound by the terms of his release, not allowed to work, not allowed to travel. Clive Wilson had told me that Biggs was often depressed, desperately touring sleazy nightclubs, boozing or high on drugs, or both, which served only to deepen his melancholia.

Although he had acted out his chirpy chappie routine during the interviews, the forced cheerfulness did slip from time to time, especially as drinking heightened his nostalgia. As we continued to down beers, with me doing my utmost not to keep up with him, he began to tell me how much he missed England – little things, like going to the pub, eating Mars bars, even buying brown sauce.

'Do you know how much a bottle of fucking HP sauce costs

here? Six bastard dollars!' I nodded sympathetically. 'And you can't get a decent bloody cup of tea anywhere. I tell you, sometimes I feel like turning myself in.'

That came like a bolt from the blue. In the circumstances, I hardly dared to take the subject up, but clearly some response was needed.

'Why don't you?'

Biggs took another swig at his beer. 'I've thought about it a lot,' he said, 'ever since I had it on my toes out of Wandsworth. There was no way I was ever going to do my full stretch. Everybody knows thirty years was a diabolical liberty. For what! Robbing a fucking train. We didn't commit murder. There was no violence, not really. What there was, was an accident. If it had been twenty, say, I'd have done my time, if I'd had something to look forward to, seeing my wife and kids again, my mates…'

Ronnie took another couple of bottles out of the refrigerator. I sipped slowly at mine and watched as Ronnie downed half the bottle with a single gulp.

'But it's all changed now,' he went on. 'They'd be glad to see me back. 'Course I'd have to do a few years bird but I can do that. Even Wandsworth is a bleeding holiday camp after serving time in prison here. I've got support back home,' he continued, convinced by his own argument. 'I'm a reformed criminal, I could be a sort of role model. I could help to train today's youth, know what I mean?'

All I knew was that Ronnie was well and truly drunk by now, though he showed no sign of wanting to stop drinking. I also knew I needed to get myself out as soon as possible but Ronnie had the bit between his teeth now; he just wanted to ramble on. Going to a wall rack full of records he showed me the one he had made with the Sex Pistols, 'Cosh the Driver', which was banned from British radio. Very tasteless and hardly likely to appeal to the British public. Ronnie laughed it off.

'I needed the money,' he said: obviously his excuse for everything. 'They also wanted me to do one called "Belsen was a Gas". They sold millions. That fucker Malcolm McLaren owes me thousands!'

Again I felt I had to get out of there but there was still something to do. I tried hard to concentrate, the drink was beginning to affect my judgement.

My mind soon sharpened up as suddenly, for no reason, Biggs went on to talk about the events of the failed kidnap attempt two years ago. Was Biggs as drunk as he seemed, or was he testing me? Wilson had introduced me, after all, just as he had Miller and the others. The connection made me feel uncomfortable.

Of course I knew exactly what had happened, probably better than Biggs did, and more about the characters involved, especially Fred and big John. I decided to stay blank, as though I knew nothing about the details of the story, and restricted my comments for fear of letting slip that I knew more than he did.

It was a relief when we were interrupted by the arrival of his son, Michael, presumably back from school, accompanied by a smiling middle-aged woman who seemed to be a child-minder. Michael was seven years old now and clearly had a great love for his father who, after all, had practically brought the boy up while his mother was on her world tours. Biggs' face lit up too as the boy jumped on his lap and he introduced him with pride. He had good reason to be attached to the nice kid, however, quite apart from fatherhood, since it was Michael's birth that had helped win him his freedom in Brazil.

Ronnie insisted that I take photographs of him and the boy, posing on the big sofa. Then the bell rang and two friends arrived, an Englishman, John Pickston, with his Brazilian wife, Lea. They also frequently looked after young Michael, who was plainly on terms of intimacy with them: I guessed Lea was a surrogate mother.

John Pickston struck me as strange and evasive when I tried to make small talk with them, while still planning how to make my getaway. I had no doubt that Pickston was a pretty shady character: within minutes he was trying to flog me some emeralds, probably with a provenance just as shady.

Michael was getting excited now, running around the apartment shouting and laughing: it was time to make my play before going back to the hotel.

'I'll leave you with your friends, Ronnie,' I said, 'but you will say hello to my wife when she arrives, won't you? She's dying to meet you.'

I'd mentioned my wife's arrival earlier, over lunch, the story being that she was thrilled to be visiting Rio, and that I hoped Ronnie would introduce us to some of the city's sights.

The strategy worked well: it was not difficult to tickle Ronnie's ego. He had talked about taking us to the *Desfile* performance being held the following Monday at the Sugar Loaf Mountain, the *Desfile* being a show given by the Samba school that had been adjudged the best at Rio's famous Carnival. Ronnie, of course, had made it clear that the tickets were expensive and hard to come by and that I would have to shell out for them.

To tell the truth, I didn't particularly want to see a bunch of over-costumed dancers and transvestites prancing about but it gave me the opportunity to suggest another meeting, the day before the *Desfile*, when we could all have dinner at the Churrascaria, the restaurant where I first made contact with Biggs.

'OK, mate, you're on.'

Relieved, I said my goodbyes and prepared to leave. I was at the door, my back turned, when Ronnie called out and stopped me dead in my tracks.

'Oi! Just a minute! When did you say your wife's coming over?'

I hesitated. Had I said something to make Biggs suspicious? 'Sunday.' I replied, in as casual a way as I could manage.

Biggs guffawed. 'That's all right then. Plenty of time then to see the town – I mean see the town properly – before she comes.' He turned and winked at Pickston, who also guffawed. At least whatever Biggs had in mind was not too terrible.

'Whatever you say, Ronnie.' There were times when sucking up to this guy made me feel sick but it had to be done.

'Right, Copa tomorrow night, nine o'clock,' said Biggs briskly. 'We'll start from there.' As I nodded, smiled and turned away again, Biggs added, 'And by the way...' I looked back, wondering *What now*? 'The night's on you, right?'

I forced the smile again, not relishing yet another night of hard drinking with Biggs and his boozy hangers-on. But what the hell, mission had been accomplished. Or almost. All I had to do now was pray the others would arrive on time, decide with them what the modus operandi would be, get their agreement that the Churrascaria would be a suitable place for the snatch, and then it would be all systems go.

'See you, Ronnie,' I said and left, taking the elevator down to the ground floor. A familiar figure was seated on a bench across the road, at a distance, observing. The loyal Tony Marriage had been waiting for me to come out, watching my back all this time.

I started back to the hotel to sober up. It had been a good day.

BEHIND THE LINES

Wednesday 11th March 1981 and the *Nowcani II*, if on schedule, would be only three days from Belem. I wondered just how Miller and the others were passing their time. Big John was notorious for his high jinks and silly pranks, some of which had unintended consequences. Everything had gone remarkably smoothly so far at our end and we hoped that was also the case with Miller's team.

As I set off for my daily briefing with Tony, on Copacabana Beach, I felt very wound up and found it difficult to relax. There was still tonight to get through and there were three or four days ahead when anything could go wrong.

I arrived at the Tobruk drinks hut, our rendezvous point, but couldn't see Tony. That's odd! I thought, he's usually punctual.

'Psssst! I'm here,' called a voice, 'behind you.' I turned round and there was Tony, complete with dark sunglasses, sitting on a stone bench next to two elderly man. 'Whaddya teenk!' he asked in a mock Latin accent pointing to the washed-out blue-grey T-shirt he was wearing. 'I just got it, isn't it great?' It was a style popular with young Brazilians and 'The Chameleon' certainly looked the part. 'Remember, we're behind the lines; he whispered, in his best Sean Connery imitation, 'operating in enemy territory!' Tony was forever the joker!

There was a serious point however to Tony's joke. Now that

I was known to Biggs and his associates we had to be alert at all times. We went through the plan again, checking it over and over in our minds. Biggs would meet me and the 'wife' at the Churrascaria restaurant. If the others arrived on time, the snatch could take place there and then. That might be the easiest part, given the muscle the team possessed. Transporting the body to Belem might prove more problematic. There was still the jet to be found but I could not book for an exact date until Miller and the others were in Brazil. Then there would be the difficulty of transferring Ronnie from the airport at Belem onto the yacht. Only from then on would it be plain sailing – perhaps!

Well, the best thing to do was to take it easy for the rest of the day, to make it as uneventful as possible – and, positively, not to let a drop of liquor touch my lips! There would be time enough for that when I met Ronnie that night.

It was a great relief that Ronnie always seemed to be bang on time – probably the result of prison discipline. If it was a characteristic, and I certainly hoped it was, it would be of tremendous advantage when we went into action to make the snatch.

Biggs' punctuality was even more remarkable given that he looked and sounded sozzled. I was pretty sure too that I could smell cannabis on his breath. He declined the offer of a drink – was this a first? – but his reasoning soon became clear! Ronnie just wanted the club-crawl to begin as soon as possible.

We left the Copa on foot and headed towards the Crazy Rabbit club on Avenida Princesa Isobel. Ronnie's resolve was obviously not that strong, as we paused en route at a couple of bars. At least we did not stay too long – the pint of milk I'd drunk was already beginning to acidify – and arrived at the Crazy Rabbit where the doorman and bar staff obviously knew Ronnie well.

There was a haze of bright pink and purple coming from the lights and a strong smell of pot, which contributed to the haze along with the fumes of strong tobacco. The place was garish and seedy. As we were shown to our table, I closed my eyes several times, to accustom them gradually to the weird light.

Ronnie's groupies were there, waiting for him. Armin Heim, still clutching the airline hold-all close to his chest, was in a corner, engaged in what seemed a heated exchange with another German, an older, fatter man.

John Pickston was there with two other European men, strangers I'd not seen before, drinking beer. We sat at the table next to them and, when approached by hostesses, invited them to have a drink. I noticed the barely concealed sniggering at the next table: my impersonation of a rich mug had worked all right; they knew Ronnie would take me for a packet that evening. That was OK. That was the plan.

Ronnie was ordering beers with whisky chasers. He seemed to be on kissing terms with the waitresses and hostesses. The trick for me was to be polite but keep my distance. Diversion of any kind was the last thing I needed at this moment. Before long, Clive Wilson and a friend walked in: they were both pretty drunk. Without invitation, they plonked themselves down at our table. It was clear I was going to be the host for the evening for everybody.

'The boat's ready when you are,' said Wilson in a slurred voice. I could have hit him – the reference was to the deep-sea fishing boat I'd promised to hire but I did not want Ronnie making any subconscious connections like – Wilson – Good Time Charlie – Boat. It would be too reminiscent of the last attempt. I hurriedly arranged a lunch date with Wilson to talk over the details.

Fortunately, Ronnie was more pissed than Wilson and I were and did not seem even to notice the exchange. He and his hangers-on had all reached the noisy stage of drunkenness and were shouting ribald comments to each other across the tables. At least it prevented Ronnie from being bothered by Wilson's presence.

Armin's loud argument with his fellow German was also affording Ronnie and his chums some entertainment. The noisy altercation ended with Armin getting up and angrily and ostentatiously walking out, which action for some reason caused great hilarity among the crowd of Biggs' hangers-on. Apparently Armin was a bit of a drama queen.

The laughter turned to cheering as the floor-show was announced. Armin had just missed it. Nine beautiful golden-skinned women sashayed onto the low stage. They were not overdressed to start with but, with the full and silent attention of the audience, then began to remove the rest of their clothes. Ronnie dug me in the ribs with his elbow.

'Bet you wouldn't bring your wife to see this,' he chortled. I smiled thinly back and then watched, with wonder rather than interest, as the nine girls performed a series of lesbian sexual gyrations, culminating in a tangle of arms, legs and torsos, resulting in a kind of female Hydra, cheered on by the crowd with each successive manoeuvre in a sequence of incredible contortions.

The act came to an end while the audience applauded enthusiastically this example of both grace and physical dexterity. Ronnie and Wilson seemed to be on good terms again, sharing lewd jokes about the performers. I began to think what dick-heads they both were but then pulled myself up. I had to take Ronnie Biggs seriously at all times if we were to succeed in our venture. Time and time again he had fooled his hunters with resilience and cunning.

Ronnie continued to down endless beers, interspersed with gulps of Scotch. I merely pretended to drink gin and tonics which, in truth, were mostly all tonic and next to no gin. Following the stage show, the music had slowed from frantic samba to a more sedate tempo. One or two hostesses were dancing with their customers, others with each other. Everyone else seemed to be mumbling into their drinks, either smashed or stoned. Ronnie, who was both, had ventured onto the floor by himself, almost in a trance. He was rocking to and fro to the music, though sometimes his movements were a bit unsynchronised. His eyes were closed and he was hugging himself, as if dancing with an invisible partner.

It was time for me to slip away. I'd had enough and nobody was alert enough to register if I was missing from the party. Outside the club I breathed in great gulps of fresh air. Somewhere out there the reliable Tony was watching. But the evening was over. Thank God that there were only two days to go before the others arrived!

There was still plenty of work to do but first I had to attend the lunch arranged with Wilson at the Meridien. Fortunately, Wilson was not there – not surprisingly, given the king-sized hangover he must have had. Some of his piss-artist friends were though, and for the sake of appearances, I downed a few gin and tonics, missing out the gin, before leaving.

I headed back to the Luxor, striding along the mile-long parade for more exercise. At first, I thought maybe I was being paranoid – not unusual in the job – but then became convinced there really was someone following me. I couldn't think why. Surely Ronnie was not suspicious? Then I realised – Armin Heim had put someone on my tail. Although Biggs treated him with bored indifference, the German seemed to think he had a crucial role in protecting the fugitive.

The man was easily recognisable, not the best advertisement for a tail, but these people were amateurs. He was six foot tall, mahogany-skinned with a light streak in his dark brown hair. To cap it all, he wore the bright yellow Brazilian football shirt. Admittedly there were plenty of them around but it made it easy to keep tabs on him.

I continued my brisk stroll to the hotel, went up to my room and looked out of the window. Sure enough, the Brazilian had parked himself opposite the entrance, where he was chatting to a native in a black T-shirt.

Obviously I couldn't afford to take any chances. I phoned Tony, who had been stood down that day as Biggs was not involved, and asked him to do a check.

By arrangement, Tony was waiting in the municipal square

behind the Avenida Atlantica, a meeting place where the locals played cards and chess. It was eight o'clock. Fifteen minutes later, I walked into the square where I bought a copy of a week old English newspaper at a nearby kiosk. For five minutes, I sat on a bench and glanced through the paper, then got up and walked towards the traffic lights at the main intersection.

The man in the yellow shirt had been following me at a safe distance, distance being the operative word. I waited for a vacant taxi to stop at the lights and then, just as they were about to turn green, sprinted to the cab and jumped in, ordering the driver to take me to Ipanema.

There, just to make sure, I changed cabs and went back to the Meridien Hotel where I met up with Tony, who reported that the Brazilian had indeed been left looking silly at the kerb while the taxi shot away.

We discussed the incident and agreed it had not been particularly sinister, though it did underline that we had to remain watchful. If that was the best Armin Heim could contrive, the German was no more than a bit of a laugh.

Friday March 13th: the *Nowcani II* should have entered Para River Tributary the previous afternoon, so I called the Belem hotel twice to see if the team had arrived.

It was getting close to the attack time now and some detailed planning had to be done, so that everything was ready when Miller and crew got to Rio. The exercise was no longer a paper one but a real and risky operation. Nothing must go wrong this time. We had adequate resources, a workable plan and a dedicated and disciplined team.

D-day was set for Sunday March 15th, with the following day, Monday 16th, as a back-up date if any delays occurred. The whole operation was dependent on timings. I'd checked, for example, with the airline company who had one 6-seater Lear Jet 125D available for the weekend. The plane could not, however, take off after 11 p.m. from Santos Dumont, due to city by-laws.

'Anaconda' March 1981

Fred Prime, Patrick King, Tony Marriage and Mark Algate in Antigua

John Miller, Mark and Fred bound for Belem, Brazil

Crewman Greg Nelson checks the rigging. Thorfinn Maciver, skipper of the NOWCANI II, is at the helm

View from the Luxor Hotel on Copacabana Beach

Surveillance photo in Ronnie's favourite shop

First meeting with Ronnie by the Copacabana Palace Hotel swimming pool, 9th March, 1981

The picture that says it all: Ronnie cocking his nose at Britain!

Ronnie's luxury apartment block looks across Botologo Beach to Sugar Loaf mountain, Rio's world famous landmark

Mark Algate takes his turn at the helm - Fred Prime looks on

Relaxing below deck

Ronnie sharing a joke with his 'babysitter' Fred Prime

Ronnie with a pipe of the
'Caribbean Weed' . . .

. . . Barbados sighted after six days at sea!

Ronnie below deck writing his letter to Armin Heim before docking at Bridgetown, Barbados

John Miller marries Sarah at the Holiday Inn Bridgetown – comedian Jim Davidson is a witness

Chartered aircraft had to file take-off times with flight control and, once filed, a flight plan could not be altered without giving several hours notice, which hampered our flexibility considerably.

The flight, depending on the weather, would take about three and a half hours. The landing at Belem would have to be before 2 a.m. or after 6 a.m., otherwise special permission would have to be sought as only a skeleton staff manned the control tower. If such a request were made, a specialist technician would have to be brought in, an event that would attract unnecessary and unwelcome attention.

Even if all went smoothly with the flight, there were other factors to be taken into account. The morning tide at Belem – which it was essential to take for the *Nowcani II* to meet the ocean as quickly as possible – was at 6 a.m., which was very tight and left little time for errors or unexpected hold-ups. And what would happen if big John and his men did not arrive on time and Sunday's attempt had to be cancelled? The flight would have to be rebooked and a new schedule submitted to airport control. The worst scenario of all, of course, was if the snatch went completely wrong and the team had to make a hurried escape – there had to be a fall-back plan for that eventuality.

Tony was given the job of hiring a VW Combi minibus, using his own international driving license as proof of identity, from Telecar, a small firm on the Rua Figuerido Magalhaes. All transactions were to be made in cash and, with a substantial deposit, the hire for the weekend would be $450.

Two saloon cars were also hired privately, through the hotel's head porter, who had become well acquainted with the contents of my wallet during our stay there. The cars would be used by the members of the team as escape vehicles, should they become necessary, and they would be parked near the designated snatch point, once that was decided, with ignition keys taped to the exhaust pipes. They would contain maps of alternative routes out of Brazil, a supply of drinking water and several packs of nuts and emergency rations. Our earnest hope was that they would never be required and, as it turned out, they were not.

We then had to devise possible diversions. The plan in a nutshell was to grab Biggs in the street, throw him into the back of the Combi and restrain him until we reached the airport. Then, gagged and bound, he would be stuffed into the man-sized marquee bag the team were bringing, and carried through onto the jet.

This was Phase One, anyway. The danger period, after the snatch itself, would be walking the marquee bag through the airport. I wanted some cover for this manoeuvre, to avoid suspicion being aroused.

Tony came up with the brilliant suggestion that we should hire a couple of really stunning Brazilian models on the pretext of having a photographic session at the airport. He argued that scantily clad females in provocative poses were guaranteed to attract attention from any security guards or other petty officials.

As a contingency we would also order six cardboard cartons, containing one hundred and twenty wine glasses, as props for the models, to be built as a pyramid in the background: the idea was, if necessary, for someone to push over the stack at the right moment, the noise of breaking glass on the stone floor providing audio as well as visual distraction, while the team carried their valise across the area in the background.

Together Tony and I went to a small model agency, above Frank's Bar, near Avenida Copacabana. While Tony sought a parking spot for the car, I went upstairs. In the reception were two heavily made-up girls sitting on a long bench seat. It was a safe bet this 'model' agency was in fact an escort agency and the two ladies were obviously waiting for business. Ignoring the interest they were showing, I approached the middle-aged female receptionist.

'Do you speak English?'

'A leetle.'

'I need a couple of models to photograph at the airport. Can you supply them?'

'It's a bit public, meester,' she said, raising her eyebrows.

'No,' I said, speaking slowly, 'I don't mean for that sort of photography. I want two of your best and most attractive girls for me to photograph for a newspaper – no sex pictures!'

'OK, whatever you want. Choose from here,' she said, pushing a well-worn photo album across to me.

At this point Tony walked into the agency, saw me talking to the middle-aged receptionist and, not wanting to interrupt, sat down on the bench next to the two heavily painted women. Spotting a potential customer they immediately sidled up to him.

'Hello, meester, you want to meet me?' asked one of the girls.

'Oh, hello,' said Tony, his mind miles away. 'So what do you do for a living then?'

When I heard this ridiculous conversation, I looked round and burst out laughing, much to the annoyance of the middle-aged madam. I paid a $100 deposit for the best-looking models in the agency's album, leaving the exact timings for the session open, and then left, dragging with me a chortling Tony Marriage, who had by now caught on.

The last and most important task was to hire the Lear Jet and we drove to Santos Dumont, where the offices of the only private charter company were located.

Tony waited outside while I entered the office. The manager there had an extraordinarily big head. He was also fat and his face was badly pock-marked. It would be difficult to put anyone against him in an identity parade. On the desk in front of him was a cheap ornament, surmounted by a plastic football, about the size of a tennis ball, with BRAZIL written across it. This whole nation was soccer crazy. He was tapping his fingers on the ball – a nervous habit perhaps.

There were no jets available this coming weekend, he informed me, only a 16-seater turbo-prop. That was no good. It was slower and would have to refuel half way out: they might miss the morning tide. It was worrying but I did not panic. In this part of the world – as in many others – dollars spoke louder than words.

'Please listen,' I said, emphasising every syllable. 'I must have a Lear 1-2-5. For a film crew,' I told him, knowing the magic of the word film. 'They are very important people. Film people!'

All this was accompanied by a $100 bill which I waved to and fro. The manager's eyes followed the movement hypnotically. 'De-lay is very expensive!'

I rubbed my fingers and thumbs together emphatically, then pushed the note across the desk. The manager's fat hand, as pock-marked as his face, engulfed it as he consulted his flight diary. His fingertips went back to tapping the plastic ball as, with much sighing and shaking of his fat head, he read through the diary.

The only possible jet available was in Manaus, in the interior. I checked the layout: there were six seats in all, but Ronnie, in the bag, would take up the bench seat at the back. That left four seats for the rest – ideal. But how to get it down to Rio without breaking the bank?

The fat fingers tapped the imitation football. I made small talk for a few minutes, congratulating Brazil on being world champions. The ugly face lightened up with a smile as broad as the Cheshire cat's.

'Pele!' I volunteered, which, to tell the truth, was about the limit of my knowledge of the game.

'Bobby Moore!' exclaimed the fat man, returning the compliment. 'Bobby Charlton. Good. Good.'

Fascinating though the conversation was, I needed to get down to brass tacks. Maybe another $100 bill might do the trick.

'Maybe I move this customer here,' the manager murmured before shaking his head as though that was not really a good idea. I put the $100 on the table and almost jumped at the speed with which the greenback was snatched.

'OK,' said the man, 'OK,' which meant that the greedy fat bastard could fix it but there was still a price to be negotiated. I waved another $100 bill under his nose.

'Good price, good business,' I said, spelling out the words again. 'Understand?'

The manager understood. The $100 was delivered. Another enormous grin signified he was ready to do business. We negotiated. The charter flight to Belem cost $14,000 and I left a thousand dollars as a deposit.

I was really pleased. We had the right kind of jet for less than the budget allowed. In fact we were $2,000 to the good since I'd already allowed for the bribes. It was a result.

England one – Brazil nil.

A DOUBLE GAME

For John Miller, the voyage from Barbados had been an exhausting eight days. No seaman, he had been sick again as soon as the boat reached choppy waters and had suffered, while the others had enjoyed themselves, showing off their nautical skills.

They had been two days at sea before he felt well enough to get started on what for him was the most important task: when it came to kidnapping Ronnie, John had his own agenda. He intended to play, it seemed, a double game.

The Anaconda plan had dictated that he must take charge on the voyage back to Barbados and the thought of another week at sea appalled him.

John's vision was to be in Barbados himself when the *Nowcani II* arrived, enjoying to the full the acclaim with which they would be greeted if they had successfully pulled off the snatch.

Not for him a plan where they were all supposed to slope off quietly from Barbados before the world's press even knew about Biggs' arrival. John had always wanted to be among the celebrities himself, instead of just looking after them, and the Biggs caper could make him a star. Playing this double game, however, meant implementing measures that would change the plan in his favour without jeopardising the mission.

The most risky part of the scheme was involving Maciver somehow: his cooperation would be essential for the plan to work. How was John going to persuade the skipper into being part of the operation to capture Biggs, and when? Timing, he knew, was everything.

He didn't have to wait too long. Maciver, it seemed, was an enthusiastic amateur photographer. He had become suspicious of Fred and Mark after a few casual questions about camera work had exposed them: they were certainly not what they purported to be. Miller was an actor, who could talk his way out of just about any situation. The others came across as what they were, ex-soldiers.

Maciver had every right to be concerned. For all he knew, they were desperate criminals engaged in smuggling drugs, or drug-running, or God knows what. Although an adventurous young man, the last thing he wanted was to be involved in anything of that kind while at the start of his master's career. It is probable that Maciver had it in mind to sneak off and inform the authorities of his suspicions as soon as they reached Belem harbour.

With the so-called film crew's cover in danger of being blown, it was John who rode to the rescue, seizing his opportunity at the same time. The canny Miller was able to read Maciver's mind and guess what his intentions were. Fortunately they were on the high seas and there would be time enough to put things right. Miller never doubted his ability to manoeuvre himself out of difficult corners.

With the unerring instinct that every gambler must have, Miller knew exactly what had to be done. He told Maciver the truth, or as much of the truth as he needed to know. They were going to Brazil in order to capture a wanted criminal, Ronnie Biggs. It was an undercover operation sanctioned by the government at the request of Scotland Yard. Unbelievably, he used the old trick again of showing his passport, stating his occupation as being 'On Government Service'.

Miller smelled Maciver's excitement and decided to enrol him into the gang, on the promise of a ten grand reward if he cooperated.

With Maciver roped in, John had played a clever trick. He could not now trust Maciver to stay in Belem and so the skipper would have to accompany Fred and himself to Rio. He would also take Mark Algate, on the pretext of having him mind Maciver, to make sure he didn't slip away. With two new, unplanned for, passengers in Rio, Anaconda's transport arrangements had been scuppered.

Miller said nothing to the others about his dealings with Maciver until three days later when he told them that the captain had overheard them all talking. Nobody was surprised since they had wondered themselves why Miller had been talking openly for everyone to hear. What Miller had not realised was that Veronica Campanile, the cook, had also overheard, which could and would prove to be dangerous. The point was that everyone swallowed his story and went along with his revised plan.

It was early evening and beginning to get dark as the *Nowcani II* finished its cruise along the Para River and edged its way to the official docking point in Belem Harbour. Maciver, Prime and Miller went ashore to clear customs and navigation formalities. They were eager to hurry the process along: after their long seven and a half day voyage they wanted to hit the Belem bars and have some entertainment.

The Brazilian officials were housed in a small brick building nearby, just one large room with a few offices leading off a narrow corridor. Only two men were on duty.

The older one, a more officious character, told Maciver that *Nowcani II* could not anchor where she was and would have to travel a further two miles upstream, where the Yacht Club was situated. The crew were tired and thought their long day had finished, but at least the proximity of the Yacht Club was good news.

That was docking – now came the question of customs. The official was in no hurry to stamp the document.

'Anything to declare?' He asked. 'Any whisky?'

John got the message and sent Fred back to collect four

bottles of the best Scotch whisky from their ample stores.

Not best pleased, Fred muttered, 'I thought the piranhas were in the Amazon,' as he left.

The officials were now a lot less dour: the prospect of Scotch whisky seemed to have energised them. John joked with them while they waited and, though they could not understand a word of his accent, when he laughed, they laughed. Within ten minutes the whisky had arrived and, full of smiles now, the officers stamped the requisite papers.

They had arrived in Belem, officially.

Now that formalities had been completed, the men all went on shore leaving only Veronica, the cook, behind. By ten o'clock that night, John had rounded up a dozen Brazilian whores, presumably three each, and took them back to the boat for a party. The party was loud and wild.

The disturbance was reported and the Belem police made their arrival at the pier. A group of local men had made the mistake of trying to join the party uninvited, and Fred had laid three of them out, believing them to be robbers. Explanations were made to the police. John's gift of the gab, even when he could not speak the language, was a life-saver and, after a few sharp exchanges, everyone had calmed down.

The sun was up when the whores were finally thrown off the yacht. Veronica, the yacht's cook, had been disgusted by the men's behaviour – no one had paid any attention to her during the trip – so she decided to jump ship and find another passage home.

In the midst of the carousing she had helped herself to a few hundred dollars of Maciver's money, while he was being as drunken and dissolute as the rest of them.

The next morning, Saturday March 14th, when I rang the hotel at Belem again and this time made contact, Miller was pleased to learn that the operation had run smoothly at the Rio end and that Biggs was set up to be taken the next evening. The less time they spent in Brazil, the better it would be. John said that he and the rest were fine – and that they had all enjoyed a good night out on arriving in Belem. What he didn't say was that the voyage had not gone according to plan and events had occurred which were to have an important bearing on the way the plan would be executed. But he left that for when he and the others arrived in Rio by commercial flight the next morning.

John always believed in confessing bad news at the last possible moment.

RENDEZVOUS IN RIO

Sunday March 15th 1981, was D-day – or what I thought of later as Disaster Day!

It started when Tony rang me at the Luxor to finalise our plans. We decided it would be better if I stuck to my usual routine and turn up at the Meridien Bar at noon, to maintain our cover, while Tony collected John and Fred from Santos Dumont Airport. But where should we meet afterwards? We knew that John and Fred, after their 1979 stunt, might be recognised and had to keep as low a profile as possible. Tony had a map of Rio spread in front of him and waited while I procured my own: we spotted what appeared to be a stadium, not far from the centre.

'Look,' said Tony, 'it's surrounded by green – that must mean a park or open space. What d'you think?'

'Looks OK to me.'

We figured two o'clock would be a good time to rendezvous, allowing room for any unexpected delays. Fifteen minutes before the appointed hour I left the Meridien Hotel and caught a taxi, pointing out to the driver the place on the map. The driver seemed to look a little oddly at me, but I put it down to the fact that he was slightly cross-eyed.

The open space turned out to be anything but: it was a massive market place, crowded with Indian natives. It looked an extremely dangerous place for a foreign white man to be, quite apart from the fact that I stuck out like a beacon.

I paid the driver but, as a safeguard, asked him to wait a few minutes just in case I wanted to go back. It was a hot dusty day and there were flies everywhere, congregating in thick clouds around the butchers' stalls.

Feeling very conspicuous indeed in white polo shirt and beige shorts, I walked slowly into the market, glancing desperately around for the Combi. As a precaution, I took my watch off and slipped it in my pocket.

The deeper into the market, the worse the smell got. I could not help shuddering when I saw a hideously ugly Indian pluck a small, pathetic-looking mongrel from a wicker basket by its hind legs. In one swift and practised movement, the Indian flipped the whining creature onto a wooden block and sliced its head off with a cleaver.

This was a mad place and I reckoned it would be wise to high-tail it out of there: Tony must have got there, seen how impractical a meeting place the open space had turned out to be, and decided to beat it back to the airport.

Fortunately I caught sight of the cross-eyed taxi driver just as he seemed about to leave, sprinted over to the cab, watched with some astonishment – and a great deal of hilarity – by the onlookers, and ordered:

'Santos Dumont!'

Arriving there, my relief at seeing the team waiting by the parked minibus was cut short by the sight of Maciver and Mark Algate. What the hell were they doing there? Maciver was the skipper, for God's sake, why had Miller dragged him into this? And Mark Algate should have been the security guard on board the *Nowcani II*, making sure it did not leave for any reason until the team arrived, mission accomplished. More important, indeed crucial to the plan, Mark was to have hired a van at that end to meet the jet when it arrived at Belem. How the devil were they supposed to transport Ronnie Biggs – if all went well – to the harbour-side? Take a taxi?

I paid off the cab and, with a face like thunder, strode across to the car park. Miller saw me coming and moved quickly to intercept, before I got to the van, to explain what had happened.

The story Miller gave was that Maciver had become suspicious of Fred and Mark when he saw them handle the professional film equipment they had taken out on deck.

'You can see that, Pat, can't you? It didn't take Thorfinn too long to guess Freddie was no cameraman!'

'But I told them never to take the film equipment out, there was no need.'

'I know,' sighed John, shaking his head at their folly. 'I only noticed what they'd done at the last minute.'

Later, Fred Prime told me quite categorically that neither he nor Mark had ever touched the equipment, which had been stored in the ship's hold for the entire voyage.

John's justification for bringing Maciver with them was that he was too much of a risk to leave there, just in case he changed his mind: by coming to Rio with them, he was now thoroughly implicated. Greg Nelson had stayed alone to look after the yacht. But why had he brought Mark Algate along? Miller had no explanation other than he thought Mark might be handy to have around.

The casual Miller had dropped a megaton logistical bombshell. Arrangements had been made for four bodies plus Ronnie Biggs to be transported, and now there were six – or seven in all. The Lear Jet's configuration had only four places for passengers and a jump-seat – a folding spare for an extra airline crew-member. Even using the jump-seat and leaving Ronnie on the floor, they would be one seat short. Someone would have to travel by commercial airline and that obviously meant me.

Miller nodded in commiseration, although this, in my opinion, had been his precise intention all the way along.

I looked across at Maciver, who was feeling pretty sorry for himself. Apparently when they had driven to the market, Maciver was in the back of the minibus leaning on the side door. As the vehicle took a sharp curve on the motorway, the side doors – obviously not secured properly – had flown open and Maciver had flown out.

Fortunately he was young and fit and a former county-standard rugby player. As he hit the tarmac he had bounced back on his feet and sprinted clear. The big truck behind them had missed him by inches as it thundered past.

As I went over to check on Maciver's injuries, I thought to myself that it had not taken long for Maciver to find out that this was more than a *Boys' Own* adventure. There were risks too. While Fred, who told me the whole story later, and who resented John's having cut Maciver in on the deal, added angrily: 'Serves him right, greedy bugger!'

Events were suddenly proceeding apace and it was decided to recce the probable snatch location before nightfall. I took them off to see the luxury apartment block where Biggs was living. The van's middle seats had been stripped out, ready for its mission. It was crowded inside with everyone on board, and extremely hot.

The beach at Botafogo was about six hundred metres long, in the shape of a crescent, bordered by a promenade that rose six feet about the sand. Beyond the promenade was a busy road, divided by a central reservation about two feet wide with three-lane traffic moving on either side. The apartment building was at one end of the promenade and the Churrascaria, where Ronnie was meeting me that night, was at the other, standing just back from the road.

To go from one end to the other was hardly worth taking a taxi, it was no more than a walk. John agreed with me that it was odds on Biggs would choose to walk to the restaurant that night. If the vehicle could be strategically placed in the adjacent car park, there would be a clear field of vision, two hundred yards down the promenade.

There were also two good markers, stone benches set by the side of the road, within two hundred yards. Assuming Ronnie would be walking, when he reached the first bench the vehicle would start up and cruise along the road. Mark Algate would be seated on the second bench and, when the target approached, would stand up and block his way. Simultaneously, the van would draw up alongside, the doors would open and Biggs would be pushed by Mark, and pulled by the others, into the back of the vehicle. It would all be over in seconds.

If Ronnie did not stick to the plan, but bypassed the obstruction by arriving from another direction or in a vehicle, they would wait until Ronnie emerged from the restaurant and surprise him then. All agreed it was a feasible exercise. I signalled a cab and went back to the Luxor, where I'd already checked out that day, to pick up my luggage. I also took the opportunity to phone Jarrett in New York, the first of three important telephone calls over the next twenty-four hours which would determine the outcome of the operation. I used the simple code that was pre-arranged with Jarrett.

'The seminar's on tonight,' I told him. 'Everything's in place.'

'Splendid,' replied Jarrett, 'that's splendid.' And put the phone down. We were both men of few words.

RONNIE WHERE ARE YOU?

The dinner date with Ronnie was set for eight o'clock and the team took up its position an hour earlier, the expectation being that Ronnie would leave home some time after 7.30 p.m. and then walk down the promenade. I pointed out to them that in my experience so far, over three or four meetings, Ronnie had always been punctual.

With two extra members of the crew to fit in, there would be something of an overcrowding problem. Maciver was promoted to being the driver, as his injuries did not allow him to do much else, although Tony would take over once the snatch had been completed. I was in the passenger seat. John and Fred lay hidden in the back of the stripped down minibus. It was very hot. We were all sweating from the unbearable humidity as well as the anticipation.

The lucky ones were Mark and Tony. Mark, now wearing a long sleeve T-shirt to hide his tattoos, had taken up his place on the stone bench along the promenade. As an alternative plan, Tony had been positioned on the other side of the restaurant, in case Ronnie arrived from the opposite direction. If he did, whether he was walking or getting out of a taxi, Tony would approach him pretending to be an enthusiastic fan, maybe even asking for his autograph, anything to impede Biggs until the minibus could pull up alongside them.

By seven o'clock we were all in position and the minutes began to tick slowly by as we waited for our prey. It would soon be over.

I looked at my watch. It was ten minutes to eight. If my experience of Biggs' punctuality had been accurate, the victim should have been in view by now. Inside the van it was stuffy and unbearably hot: we were all sweating profusely from nervous tension as well as the heat.

By eight o'clock John and Fred were both getting restless. There was nothing anyone could do except wait: all the effing and blinding wouldn't make a ha'porth of difference.

'Where the fuck is he, Pat?' Miller demanded. 'Are you sure you made the arrangement for tonight?'

I didn't bother to answer.

By 8.30 p.m., we had done all the sweating we were going to do. 'Pat, for Christ sake, go in there and have a look!'

I left the van and went into the restaurant to look around, just in case Ronnie had slipped in earlier. There was no sign of Biggs and so I decided to ring him at home.

Ronnie answered the phone himself. He sounded pissed, certainly, and was probably stoned as well. His voice was thick and he was having a bout of hiccups – his mind struggled to achieve recognition of whoever was talking to him.

'Oh, fuck me, mate! Pat, I'm sorry. I forgot.' There was a long pause. 'I feel like shit. Can we make it some other time?'

What was there to say? Try to drag him out? If I was too persistent, Ronnie might smell a rat. We had another meeting planned for the next evening, when Ronnie was supposed to meet my wife. I took a chance because I was sure this was the best way to play it.

'No, that's all right, Ronnie. I can tell you're feeling a bit rough. In fact you sound fucking awful.'

The grateful chuckle at the other end told me this was the right note.

'But we'll be all right for tomorrow night, won't we? You

know my wife's dying to meet you.'

'Yeah, yeah, the *Desfile*, I'll be there. You know the gaff, don't you, on Sugar Loaf?'

'I bought the tickets, Ronnie.'

There was another laugh. The pitch was working. Ronnie believed me. 'Seven-thirty right?' I stressed.

'Seven-thirty. I'll be there chum. Don't worry.'

'Get your head down, Ronnie.'

'I will, mate, straight back to kip.'

The phone went dead at the other end and I walked back to the minibus to stand down the others.

'He's pissed. And stoned – out of his head. He was asleep, that's why he didn't come.' I waited for the expected stream of expletives to wear itself out. 'He was very apologetic. But he promised faithfully that he would be there tomorrow.'

John Miller was surprisingly quiet. He had hyped himself to such an extent that the disappointment had left him deflated. Although the rest of them felt the same way, they would have to buck up and prepare themselves for the new D-Day. There was no choice.

The first priority was to secure the Lear Jet for another twenty-four hours and so, with Tony at the wheel, we raced to Santos Dumont airport. John and I managed to persuade both the pilot and co-pilot to stay over by paying them an extra $1,000 for themselves. A further $1,000 was paid to the Lear Jet company.

Further down the terminal, were the two models, so I walked over to pay them an extra $50 each to return the following night. Next to them were the boxes of wine glasses stacked near the Varig Airlines cargo counter and I asked the foreman if he could keep them behind his counter overnight, slipping him a crisp $20 bill.

John Miller decided he and Fred should stay at the Sunshine Hotel which was out of town and near Rio's international airport. The rest of us went back to the Luxor Hotel. Ronnie not turning up had cost Anaconda an extra $2,500!*

* worth $10,000 today

Maciver needed to see a doctor as his injury was looking bad and so, now we had time to spare, I took him by taxi to the local county hospital.

Inside the large hospital building, we experienced another major culture shock. The waiting room looked like a battleground, with most of the waiting patients appearing to be victims of violence. One man had his ear missing, another had most of his sliced off, and a third had a pair of nails sticking out of his head which made him look like a cartoon Martian.

An attractive black nurse, seeing that Maciver was a foreigner, took him immediately to the treatment room on the upper floor. The room could only be reached by two large elevators guarded by armed security men. The guards were there simply to prevent family members attacking the doctors if the patient died – a common occurrence in Rio.

While Maciver was being treated, I sat in the general waiting area, watching a continuous line of wounded people arrive. One man, about sixty years old, had his hand over a bleeding hole in the front of his face, where his nose had once been. Someone had sliced it off and his young grandson had the piece of wrinkled flesh wrapped in a dirty old rag, which he kept peering at from time to time.

After about an hour, Maciver reappeared with his leg neatly bandaged and then we headed back to the Luxor. When we got there, Maciver went straight to bed to rest his injury and I went to the switchboard operators' room to call Jarrett in London.

The voice on the other end of the phone at first didn't sound particularly disappointed or worried by the news of the cancellation. The conversation, as usual, was brief.

'Tonight's seminar was cancelled.'

'What happened?'

'He was drunk, just didn't turn up.'

There was a pause and the tone in Jarrett's voice became irritable. 'He was drunk?'

'Well, that's what happened.'

'This has to be done properly. Do you understand?' he said. 'There's no more money available. This is it – the last chance. It's either tomorrow or not at all. There's no point talking now, call me when it's over.'

You bastard, I thought.

I went back to the hotel lobby to find the others. I was concerned about Tony and wanted to talk to him. His morale had dropped noticeably when Biggs failed to show up at the Churrascaria. The past ten days in Rio had shown me Tony's metal. He was a good soldier, reliable and, more importantly, I liked him. I felt confident enough in him to confide a little about Jarrett and the operation being something bigger than just getting Biggs. He had already guessed that. He had been involved in undercover work in Northern Ireland and there was a familiar feeling to the way we had been going about things.

Tony perked up after our chat and when Mark joined us in the lobby we decided to hit the local bars for a bit of relaxation. As we left the hotel Tony lifted his arms, took a deep breath, and declared 'Ah Rio! A paradise where women just flock to you.'

'Its not flockin' women I want, it's a beer!' replied Mark. His play on words made us laugh. Strangely we felt in good spirits and determined to enjoy ourselves, though our mood might have been different if we'd known what an extraordinary Monday was in store for us, on what was to be a very long day.

THE SNATCH

The next day, Monday March 16th, really did have to be D-day or it was all over. The team was ready, the guys refreshed after a good night's sleep. We had made a kind of dry run on the previous evening. It was just a matter now of everyone keeping his nerve.

It did not do my nerves any good when John Miller dropped his latest bombshell. He had decided, he told me, that after the snatch, and Ronnie's delivery on board *Nowcani II*, he would not be travelling on the yacht back to Barbados as team-leader in charge of the captive: he would leave it instead to Fred and the others.

He had suffered so badly from seasickness on the voyage out, he coolly told me, that he just could not face another six or seven days going back. Instead he would take a flight from Belem to Miami, to meet up with his fiancée.

I was stunned. The plan had always called for me to fly alone to Miami from Belem, meet up with my wife, Adrienne, then fly to Barbados posing as a couple on holiday. Once in Barbados, when I was sure the yacht was nearing its destination, I would contact the authorities and make arrangements for Biggs' arrest. As soon as the yacht arrived, Biggs would be handed over and the team would scatter to the far ends of the earth. There would be time enough later to cash in on the tremendous publicity which would surely result but, for the time being, it was to be, in army parlance, no names, no pack-drill.

It was now obvious to me that Miller had some other agenda. I had wondered what John might be up to when I phoned Adrienne at home and discovered that Sarah, John's fiancée, was accompanying her to Miami. I thought, maybe John meant to go back to Miami after Barbados for a holiday with Sarah. The last thing that crossed my mind was that John would opt out of the voyage to Barbados. Surely he would never have wanted to miss the triumph of personally handing the prisoner over to Her Majesty's representatives? It just did not make sense, though unfortunately it would in due course.

Right now I had to grapple with the problem of how to break the news to the others and, perhaps even more nerve-rackingly, to Jarrett, who, after last night, certainly would not take kindly to another change of plan – not one as central to the whole scheme as having Miller in charge on the yacht.

I knew there was no point in further pleading with John. Once Miller had made up his mind, he was as stubborn as a mule. In fact, John begged me not to tell the others.

'Look, Pat, don't tell the boys just yet. I'll do it later, when the time is right.'

It was a well-timed move. How could I risk what might be a mutiny, hours before the snatch, if I announced that the others would effectively be on their own?

There was still a couple of hours to go before the team moved into action. While they relaxed around the pool at the Sunshine Hotel, I looked for a private phone inside: with the help of a small bribe, I got the use of a room for a few minutes.

When Jarrett answered, I outlined the problem quickly and succinctly, making it clear that I had warned him Miller was a maverick, and that there was nothing I could do about that.

Jarrett listened, mostly in silence. Like me, he must have realised that at this late hour the die had been cast: the operation would either work or it would not.

Jarrett and I had never been on friendly terms, he had always kept his distance but, even so, a new coldness came into his voice. There was a hard edge to the tone and, whatever his words may have been, the message was absolutely clear. He was saying, in effect: 'Look, I put you in a position to make sure nothing went wrong. Keep to the plan and get the mark handed over to the authorities. It was always understood that this was a deniable operation. If it goes wrong, you're on your own, you know that!'

He rang off, leaving me very much on my own.

As I put the telephone down, I felt despondent and asked myself for the first time – 'What the hell am I doing here? What is going on?'

My reason for getting involved in this caper was not just for the adventure but the long term benefits. If anything went wrong now, it would all have been for nothing. It was probable that John had been working to some kind of plan of his own all along.

We'd known each other since the days of the Drum Club. I liked John. He was an entertainer, a prankster, a roistering buccaneer, the ideal man for this particular job. We had worked together before but I'd always been a bit wary of him, of his tendency to go over the top, and often take a joke too far.

But this was no joke. John had always had ambitions of being a celebrity, both Fred and I knew this and used to rib him about it. Miller thrived on notoriety and he especially enjoyed the publicity attached to the last Biggs episode. A successful attempt now would make him a star, a media personality, boasting of his adventures on an ever-revolving carousel of television chat shows. I assumed that John, with his beautiful fiancée by his side, wanted to bask in the glory of having captured Britain's most wanted criminal – there was to be no low-key voyage on the *Nowcani II* for him.

There was no point in recriminations right now. The most important thing was to get the job done.

I went to find Fred Prime to tell him the whole story, including the conversation with Jarrett, indicating that tonight was all or bust. Fred listened carefully, shaking his head from time to time in disbelief.

'I had a feeling John was up to something,' he said, 'but you know me, I'll see the job through right to the death.'

Hearing this made me feel much better.

It was decided to recce the new location in daylight. We drove to the Sugar Loaf and stared up at the cable cars – made so famous in the James Bond film – overhead. That was one hell of a dangerous looking journey!

The entrance to the cable complex, which included the Roda Vida restaurant where I was going to rendezvous with Ronnie, was entered by turning right off the one-way main road into a small square, in the centre of which was a public car park.

We found a suitable parking space among all the tourist cars and minivans, switched off and carefully surveyed the location. On the left was a small green where a war memorial had been erected. Straight ahead was a flight of steps leading to the cable complex. The entire front of it was occupied by the Roda Vida, perched on top of a seven foot high wall, decorated with plants and flowers, screening off the restaurant's patrons from prying eyes.

To the right was a military academy with two armed sentries guarding the entrance, more for military pomp than security. The academy was situated thirty metres from the main pedestrian walkway.

There were taxis dropping their passengers at the entrance to the square where the walkway began. Biggs would almost certainly arrive by taxi and, as he started along the walkway, the minibus could drive up alongside, with its doors open, and Biggs would be hauled in. Everyone agreed the plan was a practical one, but there was still some argument as to whether Roda Vida was a better bet than Biggs' apartment block.

To make sure Biggs would be coming and to find out where he would be coming from, I rang him from a nearby call-box while the gang watched and waited. Biggs came on the line.

'Hi, Ronnie, it's Pat. How're you feeling today?'

'Chipper, mate, chipper,' said Ronnie cheerfully. 'Sorry about last night.'

'That's OK. We're really looking forward to the show tonight though and the missus is so excited about meeting you.'

'That's all right, chum,' said Ronnie, in what sounded a pretty patronising way to me: obviously he was used to being taken for a celebrity. 'See you there about seven-thirty – all right?'

Without waiting for an answer he rang off. But he was coming. I hung up knowing the guys were watching my every move impatiently. So I turned and gave them the thumbs up sign. We were on!

Now that the clock was ticking, I returned to the van and we had a vigorous debate on the options open to us. Then, to make absolutely sure, we took a ride back and parked outside Ronnie's apartment. Tony, who by now knew this area well, said it was regularly patrolled by two policemen, in addition to which, there was a police post, about fifty metres behind the apartment block, manned by four officers.

Concerning the Roda Vida, there were mutterings about the proximity of the military academy and its guards, but the square and entrance to the restaurant could be full of tourists. However, we still did not know where Ronnie would be coming from.

'For God's sake, let's wait by Sugar Loaf,' said Tony Marriage, the first to take the bull by the horns. 'We know he's got to come there.'

The final decision on the four possible locations was left to John Miller as the leader of the snatch squad. Then the minibus quickly sped back to Sugar Loaf, to make sure we had a parking space well ahead of time. Luckily there was one available from which we could view the whole of the designated attack area.

We were in place in good time and, although there was still an hour to go before Biggs' estimated time of arrival of 7.30 p.m., we didn't take the chance of leaving the van in case for some reason he turned up earlier.

It was hot and humid. Inside the minibus it was like an oven, even with the windows open, and six hefty men were squashed in there, sweating profusely. Everyone's nerves were on edge.

By seven o'clock everyone was in place for the snatch and the adrenalin was flowing. The minutes ticked by like hours but eventually approached 7.30 p.m., Biggs' promised time of arrival. Everyone looked at their watches and then at me.

'He said just after seven thirty...'

No one answered. The next few minutes were the longest in my life. I still had to get to Santos Dumont where the flight plan had to be registered – or the jet would never be allowed to take off. I looked at my watch again and realised that everyone else had looked at theirs at the same time: it was like a comical piece of theatrical timing but nobody laughed. It was Tony who came to the rescue.

'Hadn't you better go, mate?' he asked. 'We don't want to miss our take-off slot.'

'Five minutes,' I replied.

'Where the fuck is he?' asked John Miller and there was a grumble of assent: that was the question everyone wanted answering.

'He'll be here,' I promised, trying to give them encouragement, though my voice was hoarse. 'This was his idea, his choice of venue. There's a big show on tonight, everyone wants to be there.'

Knowing I had to reach the Lear Jet company and file the flight plan by 8.15, I looked at my watch one last time. Was Ronnie's time-keeping going to affect the operation yet again!

'He'll be here soon, don't worry,' I said, looking at the faces in the minibus. I jumped out and hailed a taxi for the airport.

While I was being driven to Santos Dumont to do what had to be done there, a mood of near anarchy erupted in the van. To relieve their own frustrations, they cursed and swore, and even started to discuss when John would call the whole thing off. Luckily military discipline prevailed and they at least remained alert and ready to accomplish their mission – if it were at all possible.

At 7.55 p.m., when the mark finally did arrive at Sugar Loaf, they were ready, but he was fortunate: that lucky star of Ronnie Biggs' was still shining down. The taxi he was in arrived at the entrance behind a coach that was disgorging a load of tourists and, as the cab came to a halt, another coach drew up behind and quickly started to empty its load too.

The team looked on in disbelief as the mark was immediately engulfed in a jostling throng, trying to make their way in. Their chances of a snatch at that precise moment in time were exactly zero! Biggs could just be seen walking up the stairs and entering the restaurant.

'Lucky bastard!' said someone.

John Miller took charge at once. This was what he was good at, thinking fast, going into action.

'Look,' he said, 'we can't let him get away. This is our last chance. It's as simple as that.'

At least Ronnie was clearly in view, sitting at a table near the entrance, overlooking the square. He would still have time, though, to recognise anyone approaching him, and sound the alarm. That ruled out John and Fred, who were well known to their intended victim, and the lumbering Fred Prime was not equipped for a sprint like this one anyway. Had the snatch been from the roadside, as anticipated – the scenario would have been different. It was a time for improvisation. Fortunately they had done their preparations well in studying the lie of the land.

'No point in fucking around,' said Miller incisively. 'You two just go in there, get a stranglehold on him, the other one grab his legs. Carry the bastard out and don't let anyone get in your way. Fred and I will be waiting to sling him in the van and truss him up. Just do it, bang, bang, bang. In ten, fifteen seconds it will all be over and most people won't even know what's happened. Are you ready?'

'Let's do it, Mark,' said Tony.

'Go!'

The doors were thrown open and Mark and Tony walked swiftly up the stairs and entered the restaurant. Waiters were carrying trays of plates and glasses: the place was getting really busy. Ronnie was seated nearby, browsing through a magazine.

He did not even notice the stranger who brushed by his shoulder – it was Tony identifying Biggs for Mark.

Tony waited for Mark to make his move. He saw him approaching Biggs' table, eyes focussed on his prey, relentless in body language as a stalking leopard. At the same time, an elderly waiter came into view, carrying a full tray, heading in the same direction. The unsuspecting train robber was just lifting a glass to his mouth, already savouring the bouquet, anticipating another good, buckshee night on the tiles.

Suddenly he was seized from behind in a tight half-Nelson hold. As he was forced back in his chair, he kicked out, upsetting the table with its bottles and glasses. Tony Marriage grabbed Ronnie's legs and held onto them, vice-like. The momentum of the three men carried them towards the steps at the exit, across the path of the elderly waiter, who was sent flying along with the contents of his tray.

They continued to barge their way out. One diner's face finished up being squashed into his plate. Biggs' flapping hands, grasping at anything that might prevent their progress, caught hold of the corner of a table but only fastened onto the tablecloth, yanking it clean off, together with its complement of plates and glasses.

As they reached the head of the steps outside and looked for any opposition, they only saw everyone frozen as if caught by a camera, mid-action, silent and motionless, like the stop-frame of a film.

Miller saw them emerge and he and Fred tumbled out of the van, making for the action, the Scotsman leaping up the stairway to meet the others, Fred trailing in his wake. Biggs began shouting for help in Portuguese, *'Ajude-me! Ajude-me!'* The gang only yelled back at him, laughing uproariously, giving the appearance of drunken tourists. All four hoisted him unceremoniously into the back of the van. For a moment, Ronnie was able to get his arms free and grab at the sides of the doors but a swift downward chop from Fred soon made him let go. The doors were slammed shut.

It was all over in sixteen seconds.

Tony Marriage pushed Thorfinn out of the driver's seat and took over. Carefully, at no great speed, with no wheel spin, he took off. It had all happened so fast that most of the people around the restaurant precinct were probably unaware that anything out of the ordinary had taken place. A waiter had dropped a tray with plates and glasses crashing to the floor. Three obnoxious drunks, probably Americans, had staggered down the steps. There was nothing remarkable about a tourist minibus driving off.

His face pushed down on the floor to smother his shouts for help, Ronnie's hands were tied behind his back and then his legs were bound together. Only then did they turn the victim over, face up, when, even in the dim light, he recognised his kidnappers.

'Fuck me!' were his first words, 'Not you again, Fred!'

'Hullo, Ronnie,' a familiar Scots brogue intoned. 'Yes, it's me again.' The image of John Miller loomed over him. 'We've waited a long time for this.'

Strangely enough, knowing the identity of his kidnappers seemed to calm Biggs down: after all, they were all on first-name terms.

'Don't tie me up too tight,' was all he said.

Quietly and in a friendly manner, Miller outlined what was now going to happen. Ronnie was going to be put in the marquee valise, lying beside him like a canvas coffin, and he would have to stay there for about five hours.

They would make his journey as comfortable as possible, so long as he cooperated. If he didn't? The huge, jolly Fred beamed as he smacked a giant fist into his palm to demonstrate. Ronnie smiled thinly and nodded.

Outside a siren wailed loudly and for a second the former soldiers instinctively froze, fearing the worse. But the police car hurtled past and an audible sigh of relief was heard.

As the van sped – within speed limits, of course – to Santos Dumont, the men in the back went about their work.

ANACONDA – LIVE SPECIMEN

When I got to the Lear Jet office at Santos Dumont airport, the fat-faced manager was not on duty. His replacement, however, had been expecting me, and we exchanged the usual pleasantries. I wasn't able to give an exact time of arrival and because I wanted to get the flight plan filed, I told the representative the team would be on board by nine o'clock, praying that would be the case. He telephoned the control tower and the flight plan was logged. Thank God for that. I then explained the crew were carrying a sedated reptile in a bag, which they needed to take in the cabin, not in the hold. I made gestures with my arms indicating the creature was small, I didn't want to alarm the man. I don't think he really understood me and just shrugged his approval. Finally, just before leaving I asked if he could accompany the film crew from their vehicle to the plane to help make a quick departure. He nodded.

Leaving the Lear Jet office, I went across to the terminal to the Varig cargo office at the airport, trying to stay inconspicuous. From where I stood at the counter, I could see the two models waiting by the table with the wine glasses, impatient to start their photo-session.

I tried to keep out of sight because the last thing I wanted at this moment was for them to come and start twittering over me. I felt tense and wound up waiting for the minibus to arrive. From my vantage point I could see where the van would park by the kerbside, about fifty metres away and to the left. To my right, a little further away, were two frosted-glass doors, monitored by an armed security guard. This was the entry to the private jet area where the team would have to enter, lugging the Anaconda bag.

The guard, who was bored, kept glancing across at the models, which at least meant that the diversion had a good chance of working. But where was the van? It was now 8.45 p.m. The tension was becoming unbearable. What had happened? Had Ronnie failed to turn up again? Was the operation going to be another dismal failure? Or had he arrived and they had failed to grab him? If that was the case, had they managed to get away, or had they been arrested? What should I do about my flight to Miami?

At 8.46 p.m. the minibus drew up at the kerbside.

John Miller got out, followed by Fred and Mark. They stayed guard by the vehicle while the two inside kept an eye on Ronnie. Miller walked slowly and deliberately towards the glass doors and, when barred by the security guard, merely asked where the private jet office was. The guard saluted him and pointed the way.

With his usual jaunty air, John entered the office, shook hands with the company representative and the pilot who were waiting for them, and refused the offer of a cup of coffee. He went through the practised routine of his documentary film crew scenario and explained about the sedated anaconda in the bag, which he would like to get on board as soon as possible. Permission was granted and he returned to the van.

Their live cargo was already prepared to be taken into the airport: Ronnie, bound and gagged inside the bag. A label, composed in Letraset, had been pinned onto the bag, it read: 'Anaconda, Live Specimen'. Ronnie could see nothing but could hear. He guessed they were at an airport by the sounds outside. The next thing he knew he was being lifted, tilted, handled outside the van and then dumped onto the roadside. It was concrete and it hurt. He grunted.

Miller and Prime took the front handles of the valise and Algate and Marriage the rear ones. Maciver was left to lock up the van. The bag, though bulky, looked as though it contained a very strangely shaped anaconda, so Marriage slung a coil of rope on top to break the contours.

The men proceeded on their journey, walking calmly across the terminal. Then Tony stumbled and let his corner slip. He caught the bag just before it hit the floor and there was a muffled groan from within as the representative from the airline approached them. For a moment my heart seemed to stop beating, and then I was able to start breathing again as the airline man ushered the perspiring gang and their strange cargo past the interested security guard, through the waiting area and on to the tarmac. Maciver followed in their wake.

The captain was waiting to greet them at the plane, at the foot of the short stairway. Miller nodded him aside and gestured Tony to accompany him aboard. Then, wedged in the narrow opening, they pulled as Fred and Mark heaved the heavy valise up the steps. For Ronnie Biggs it must have been a really bumpy ride.

It was impossible for the five burly Britons to stand upright in the cramped interior and so everyone had to move around doubled up. The valise was dumped heavily across the back bench seat, barely six feet wide. John and Fred occupied the pair of seats nearest to Ronnie, with Thorfinn and Tony in front. The captain was not best pleased to see one of his passengers, Mark Algate, occupy the fold-down jump seat, normally reserved for crew, but he was not going to get into an argument with this crowd and went forward to the flight deck.

I watched from the airport and heaved a deep sigh of relief as the jet hurtled down the runway and smoothly lifted into the air. Phase one had been completed successfully at least. Now it was a matter of getting the anaconda on board the

Nowcani II, though there were still plenty of possible dangers ahead.

I was wondering what was happening back in Rio? Was anyone aware that Ronnie had been kidnapped, or did the incident pass off as a drunken brawl? How had Ronnie's friends reacted when he did not turn up for the show? Had anyone checked his apartment? More importantly, had anyone called the police?

There was still time for the police to put two and two together and be waiting at Belem for the jet to arrive. There also remained the problem of unloading the anaconda and transferring it to the boat without arousing suspicion. The transport we'd planned was now not waiting at the other end. The Amazon was not exactly the place you could hire vehicles at two o'clock in the morning. The team would have to improvise some way of getting their load from Belem airport to the Yacht Club.

There was nothing more I could do. It was down to John and the others now.

There would be no John once Ronnie had been taken on board. It would be Fred's responsibility to keep Ronnie in check once they had set sail for Barbados. While I trusted Fred implicitly, Ronnie's trickery was legendary. But what could he do to escape except swim with the sharks?

There was still the possibility of a coastguard vessel going after them. They would not be legally safe until they had reached international waters. Until then they were in deep trouble. The story of it being a publicity stunt would no longer work for them.

It was all too much to think about. I would know how it went when John Miller arrived in Miami – but even then it would all be far from over.

With a sigh, I checked that my flight to Miami was on time, then went to pay the models and call off the photo-shoot.

FEAR OF FLYING

They should have been able to relax. It should have been an experience, flying by private jet the way rich people do, or real film crews on big feature films, but the nervous tension had not eased.

Outside, it had been hot and humid. Inside, they were still sweating, even with the air-conditioning operating at refrigeration level, drying out the perspiration on their faces, leaving a chill.

As the jet lifted off the runway, there was a combined sigh of relief. Each member of the team sat silent, deep in his own thoughts.

For Tony Marriage, the only member of the team to have been in all phases, there was a feeling of achievement yet trepidation. It was like scoring a goal but not yet winning the game, he thought.

Still they could not relax, not entirely. Only Fred seemed quite unperturbed: he was busy tucking into prawn sandwiches and champagne, thoughtfully provided by the airline. The others seemed to have lost their appetites.

Miller was aware of sound and movement behind him and he looked at the bag. There might have been a real live anaconda in it, the way it moved, but there were distinct groans. Either Biggs had managed to free himself partially and was trying to cry out, or he was having a fit of some kind! Ronnie was healthy enough for a man of his age, considering the way he abused himself with drink and drugs, but he had suffered a rough journey. He had been grabbed, gagged and tied up, stuffed in a canvas bag which in itself must have been a stuffy experience, thrown about in the back of the van, hauled across the airport concourse – being dropped on his arse en route, pushed and pulled up a flight of stairs and then dumped down again – all in the course of a couple of hours! It would not be surprising if he had been affected for the worse.

Calling on the others to provide cover for him, to shield him from the vision of the pilot, Miller went back to investigate. Ronnie had managed to loosen his bonds and was trying to get at his gag. Miller soon quietened him but Ronnie's body was still twitching, involuntarily it seemed, and he was icy cold. It must have been like a coffin in the bag.

Whispering instructions to Mark to make sure that Ronnie was securely taped again, Miller made his way to the front of the plane to request that the air-conditioning be turned down. The pilot must have thought it a strange request but obliged.

This time Tony, who was a trained medic, went to check on Biggs. He found Mark had done his work. Biggs was certainly not going to be able to break out of the bag but he was still cold. Tony left the bag partially open to allow Biggs some fresh air. He diagnosed that Ronnie was probably in slight shock but a fit man and there was no danger.

The jet landed at Belem in the early hours of Tuesday morning, March 17th. The airport was virtually closed since there was no flight scheduled till 6.30 a.m. The group still had to transport themselves and their anaconda to the *Nowcani II* but, of course, they had no vehicle. There was a line of taxis, old beaten-up VW Beetles, just outside the terminal but the drivers had all gone to sleep, not expecting any business.

John surveyed the line and thought: Right, that's the way we'll have to go. First though he did a quick check on their captive, who was quiet and still breathing. Ronnie had seemingly recovered from the malady he had suffered during the flight, probably the result of shock setting in after the traumatic snatch incident.

Relieved – it would have been an awfully wasted journey otherwise – John and Fred went to bang on the windows of the VWs at the front of the line, probably causing a few cardiac arrests in the process. Three of them were commandeered, the first one taking the unfortunate Ronnie squashed across the rear bench seat with Fred Prime on the edge. Ronnie was awake by now and uncomfortable. As the taxi driver simultaneously switched on the engine and the radio, from his canvas cell he could hear the call-sign of Radio Belem.

The driver was immediately ordered to turn the radio off, but Ronnie now knew exactly where he was, much further from Rio than he had expected – in fact already a third of the journey back to Wandsworth Prison, if that was to be his eventual destination.

The others piled into the back of the next two taxis and the convoy set off for the Yacht Club at Belem but, when they got there, that too was closed. The gates were locked and barred.

Luckily there were no witnesses to their arrival, once the taxi drivers returned to the airport. There seemed to be no night-watchman and the place was deserted. But they had to get inside somehow and down to the pier, to get Biggs out to the boat. There was no alternative but to climb over.

Easier said than done: the gates were seven feet high, fortunately with no spikes on top. Again military training took over. Tony was ordered to climb to the top and, sitting astride, help the others up – first Mark and then the injured Thorfinn, who still had his leg bandaged from the accident. Mark, from the other side, then helped Thorfinn down.

Sweltering in the tropical heat, it needed all the strength the two big men could muster to heave the heavy bag up to Tony, who then had to manoeuvre it over the top and lower it to Mark and Thorfinn to take the weight.

Poor Ronnie must have thought that his journey of torture

had finally concluded, only to be heaved into the air like a sack of coals, slung over some painful obstruction, then lowered head down until at last he was deposited on the ground.

Biggs was carried to the waterfront. They hoped to find a craft to take them to the *Nowcani II*, moored about a hundred yards out but there was nothing there. The Yacht Club was closed, locked up, deserted, so they resorted to standing at the water's edge, yelling across to Greg Nelson, the crewman who had been left in charge. So there they were, shouting at the tops of their voices to attract attention to themselves, the last thing they needed with the world's most wanted criminal wriggling about in a bag at their feet.

'It's no good,' said Miller eventually, calling a halt to their efforts. He turned to the resourceful Marriage. 'You'll have to swim out there, Tony.'

Even the intrepid Tony Marriage blanched at the thought of diving into the black waters of the Amazon, inhabited by piranha and caymans but, like a good soldier, he was ready to obey. This proved unnecessary however, as Greg Nelson had been woken from their cries. He climbed from the cabin onto the deck and looked across to see what the hullabaloo was all about. Miller shouted for him to bring the dinghy across. Greg raised a hand in acknowledgement.

The dinghy was a ten foot inflatable with just enough room for John and Fred, the marquee valise, and Greg to operate the outboard engine. Halfway across, Miller untied the bag. He and Fred had had quite enough of shunting Ronnie Biggs' body around, he could get himself on board.

It did not enter Miller's mind at the time that no one had told Greg Nelson, the eighteen-year-old from North Carolina, what this trip was all about: he still thought they were a film crew who had gone to Rio to pick up some equipment.

'Holy shit! A body!' he exclaimed, as Ronnie rose up from the canvas bag, and almost fell off the dinghy into the Amazon. John gave a brief explanation as they completed their journey and, by the time they reached the *Nowcani II*, the young man was hooked.

The American boy, who might have been expected to make a run for it to tell the police when they went ashore again to collect the others, was so awestruck by big John's lucid prose that the first thing he did when he arrived back on board was to request a photograph of himself with the great Ronnie Biggs.

Ronnie took it all surprisingly well and, when his gag and tapes were removed and he was able to get his circulation running again, without too much recrimination. They had prepared for his reception of course and there was an ample supply of beer as well as brandy, of which Ronnie was inordinately fond. If their prisoner was going to be sozzled throughout the voyage, and consequently placid, this would suit them very well. What really did the trick, however, was when Thorfinn slapped a plastic bag of top quality grass on the table: that was what Ronnie's shattered nerves were dying for. He was still obviously suspicious of Mark and Tony, particularly Mark, who had grabbed him in the restaurant, but was friendly enough with Fred. Even given the strange circumstances, both men genuinely liked each other.

The captive drank three cold beers in quick succession followed by a large brandy chaser and soon began to relax. Then Miller, inexplicably, revealed the plan to Biggs, possibly to pacify him. He explained that once they got to Barbados, Charmian and the kids would be there waiting. Biggs of course didn't believe him. 'You lying bastard!'

'Honest Ronnie,' protested John 'they'll be there.'

Ronnie did not like Miller. Not any more. He had found him entertaining enough that first time John had come to Brazil, but now he had changed his mind. Years later Ronnie was to say, in his autobiography, that he had never ever thought of being violent in his career, but that he would cheerfully have killed Miller at that moment. He was not looking forward to spending a long sea voyage with the man but he might be able to push him over into the shark-infested waters, he thought grimly. After all, they could not possibly harm him, he was too important. He was the prize they had come to Brazil for: yes, he would kill Miller all right!

Ronnie never had the chance. Miller was about to leave the yacht and he wasn't going to let anyone interfere with his plans. He went from one to the other of his companions in the enterprise, telling each a marginally different story, the burden of it being that some time that morning Ronnie was going to be missed, if he was not already, and enquiries would be made. Because of the 1979 attempt he would of course be a suspect, so what he needed to do, John said, was to be somewhere else and take the heat off the team. He would go to Barbados and wait their arrival.

They were all too tired and stunned by the night's events to take in exactly what Miller was really saying. Only Fred knew it was a downright lie because he'd already been warned that John had no intention of making the voyage to Barbados. He said nothing to John, who left him in charge, but he felt really betrayed because he knew there was no need for Miller to be in Barbados.

Miller solemnly shook hands with everyone on the boat, barring Ronnie, who was now asleep. He scribbled a message on a piece of old notepaper and handed it to Tony Marriage. 'Show this to Ronnie tomorrow.' Tony read the letter which underlined John's promise to Biggs of having Charmian and the kids waiting in Barbados. As he stepped onto the dingy John looked back at Tony and said: 'On second thoughts just throw that fucking note away.' Tony never did deliver the note.

It was now four o'clock and Miller's flight from Belem airport to Miami was at six. He left, totally unaware that the *Nowcani II* had a broken component and would not be able to sail that day – a mishap that could have cost everybody on board the yacht dearly.

AMAZON

Fred Prime was supposed to be in charge, but what that meant was that he was in charge of Ronnie Biggs. The person responsible for getting *Nowcani II* from Belem to Bridgetown was Thorfinn Maciver. It had been a big day for him when, at the age of twenty-five, he was made Captain of an ocean-going yacht. He hadn't imagined then that he would ever be responsible for a gang of desperados transporting to Barbados a wanted criminal they'd snatched in Brazil. Months later, Maciver told me that he began to suspect that Miller's departure had been pre-planned, even on the way over, and that was the real reason he'd been taken into Miller's confidence.

It was five-thirty in the morning when Maciver ordered his young crewman, Greg Nelson, to make ready to depart. The skipper, however, was having trouble starting the engine and went below to investigate. To his horror he found the generator was not working, it had a defective component. The electricity they were currently using was being powered by the emergency batteries, which had kicked in automatically.

Ronnie Biggs seemed to be the least of all their worries. Even though he did not know his eventual fate, the worst it could be was a return to Wandsworth – and he had resigned himself to that eventuality long ago. He appeared quite happy chatting to Fred, smoking grass and drinking brandy by the bottle.

There was only one thing he seemed really worried about, and that came up every so often, when he was conscious. He and Fred pretty well went through the same dialogue routine:

'You sure my Michael's all right, Fred?'

'Course he is. I told you. We never saw him. We never touched him.'

'You sure about that, Fred?'

'Honest, Ronnie. I give you my word.'

And then he would go back to the bottle.

By six-thirty, when the dawn sun broke through, lighting up the Para River, Maciver was exhausted and his leg injury still troubled him enough to wince every time he climbed the stairs.

The yacht's generator was cutting out frequently and still would not start the engines. Without engine power he couldn't steer the sixty foot yacht through the rapid currents of the Para River.

Ronnie had drunk himself to sleep, which had allowed his guards, Fred and Tony, to doze off fitfully while Mark took his turn on watch. They were all concerned when Thorfinn told them they had missed the morning tide and would now have to wait till night-time – assuming he could find and fit a replacement for the defective generator.

This twelve hour delay in setting sail had them all nervous, especially when they realised the possible consequences. Every minute *Nowcani II* remained in Belem was a minute nearer discovery. Whispering amongst themselves, they agreed that no one would tell Ronnie there was any problem: they would make the waiting appear to be all part of the plan. In fact, if they could keep him in his present state, he would never even notice they had not moved. The curtains over the portholes in Biggs' cabin remained drawn.

They looked across at the shore where the daily routine of the marina was already under way. Soon the port officials would be arriving for work. Maciver would have to go ashore shortly to make certain he would be able to find the faulty component. But anything could happen in that time.

Fred was worried by doubts about Maciver. For a start, how did they know that his story about the generator was not baloney? None of them were ship's mechanics. What if, now that John had skipped it, Maciver lost his bottle and was planning to go ashore to report them to the police? He could always come up with some cock-and-bull story about being press-ganged into joining them.

They agreed they would keep an eye on him. But it was not Maciver that they were principally worried about. Tony Marriage was the first to express their fears.

'Listen, we could easily be traced. It can only be a matter of time before they realise Ronnie's been taken, if they don't already...'

'And that's going to ring a few bells, like who tried it on before – and how?'

'Right. If the police aren't thick, they'll soon check the airline...'

'Get a description of us with this bloody great bag...'

'The anaconda story's never going to wash.'

'That gets them to Belem. They know the time. They've only got to talk to the taxi drivers.'

'And we're here, sitting ducks!'

It was a sobering thought. They decided to send Tony across with Thorfinn, as a minder, when he went ashore. If it needed an excuse, Tony could take a load of whisky to keep the customs people happy.

Maciver was at the Yacht Club's repair shop, closely attended by Tony Marriage, when it opened at eight o'clock. Although they did not stock the particular component Maciver wanted, he bought another couple of items. He thought he might be able to fix the problem, temporarily at least: with luck it would give them enough power to travel the ninety miles to the Atlantic Ocean.

On Tuesday March 17th, just before 6 p.m., the *Nowcani II* upped anchor and glided out of the harbour. She was going well but Thorfinn soon realised his quick repair was not going to last that long.

He decided that he had no option but to use all available power to drive the engine hard and make full speed to get clear of Brazilian waters, which would take about twenty-four hours. He had heard the others muttering and was just as alarmed as they were at the prospect of being caught. In fact he admitted to himself he was shit scared and wished he had never got involved in this caper.

He relaxed only when, a day later, they reached international waters – just in time! As if on cue, the generator packed up again, this time for good.

From now on, the voyage was going to be a test of seamanship – just wind and sail.

PIRATES OF THE CARIBBEAN

It had been 9.30 p.m. the previous evening when I jumped into a cab at Santos Dumont, having seen the plane take off safely, together with the prisoner. Everything had run a little later than planned but, after a hectic dash of forty minutes, I arrived at Rio International Airport just in time to buy a one-way ticket to Miami.

Once in Miami, I switched to an Air Florida flight to Key West, and arrived about twelve noon. I booked into the Ramada Inn, and met up with my wife, Adrienne. She had flown out to Miami with Sarah, John Miller's wife-to-be, at Sarah's request – again, no doubt part of John's planning, although no one really knew, not even Sarah.

At least the project seemed to be running OK. The *Nowcani II* should be comfortably away by now, I thought, although without Miller. I spent the afternoon telling the two women about everything that had happened down in Rio, and then we all went to the airport in the evening to meet John.

Of course I realised that the adventure was far from over. But at least the *Nowcani II* was now en route for Barbados: I felt quite sure the prisoner would be safe and well, and as young Maciver had steered them safely across to Belem, presumably he'd have no problems getting back to Bridgetown.

There was always the worry that the police might have mounted a hunt for the kidnappers and, if there had been unforeseen delays, could still catch up with them. But what worried me most was exactly what game John was playing.

I couldn't believe that John would make contact with the press – that had been why he had goofed on the previous mission – but now the *Nowcani II* was Barbados bound, would he be able to resist the temptation?

On board the *Nowcani II*, Biggs had been ordered to stay in his cabin – until they reached international waters, although he was not told that. He was remarkably relaxed for the victim of a kidnap. Perhaps it was a result of long spells as a guest in Her Majesty's prisons; perhaps even a kind of philosophy he had picked up from his Christian Science friends in Rio; or, more likely, the free and plentiful supply of good liquor and top of the range marijuana – whichever way, he seemed unfazed by his experience and gave no trouble to his captors.

Fred, who had at first taken to guarding the door of the cabin, standing at ease as if he had been on military duty, was also relaxed now. He had always felt friendly towards Ronnie, although he never let his feelings stand in the way of what he considered to be his duty, namely to capture a prisoner and then escort him to a designated destination.

Fred and Ronnie had struck up a rapport from the moment they had first met. Although Ronnie was older, they were both products of the same South London working class environment: they spoke the same language. It had taken all of Fred's time serving with the Scots Guards for him to understand their foreign accent. So, now they were safely under way, he was quite happy, while restricting Ronnie in his movements, to keep him happy, have a chat and a few beers with him. He did draw the line at sharing his marijuana habit however.

'Go on, Fred, have a pipe, it'll be an experience for you. Or I'll roll you a joint if you like…?'

'Ronnie, I keep telling you… I don't smoke, never have smoked, and never will! – So leave it out!'

* * *

The celebration dinner had passed off reasonably well. John was in exuberant spirits as always and kept us rocking with laughter as he took up the story where I left off, with the jet taking off for Belem.

Although he had been quite a bit worried about Ronnie's well-being in the course of the flight, now it was all over and the prisoner had been transferred successfully to the boat for his journey to Barbados, John could stick to the more comic aspects of the tale.

We all had a good laugh, loudly enough to turn the heads of the other diners. John was a good actor and mimic and he did a terrific comic performance playing the part of Ronnie Biggs rising like a zombie from the interior of the bag, causing the unsuspecting Greg to almost fall off the dinghy.

He made a great tale too of their arrival at Belem, calmly thanking the captain for a good flight, realising that they had no transport and that the taxi drivers were all fast asleep. He gave a hilarious impression of a Brazilian taxi driver being rudely woken up in the middle of the night, thinking he was being mugged and then, when he had got over that shock, being asked to take a dangerous anaconda across the back of the rear seat of his cab.

His account of the problems that confronted them when they got to the Yacht Club, all locked up and without a soul in sight or hearing range, were just as funny. Yet somehow they had to get past the locked gates and the high fencing, not only by having to climb up and scramble over themselves but also to manage to manhandle the bulky valise and the body inside it which groaned and made muffled curses every time it took a bump, which was frequently, both on the way up and then the way down.

It was a good story, well told, and in spite of my previous worries, I began to think that maybe it would all work out according to plan. Retelling the events, having a good laugh over them now that the very real danger had passed, left me feeling quite optimistic.

The following morning I went to see if John wanted to go down to breakfast with me. I heard John's voice, so I knocked and entered. He was on the phone. talking to someone about Biggs' whereabouts. There was no doubt in my mind about who the someone was – the tabloid press. John had done it again.

He cut short his conversation and rang off guiltily. As soon as I confronted him John blustered excuses in his usual way. He had called no one, he said, the *Sun* had called him: he didn't explain how the *Sun* could possibly have known where he was staying in America. Or had they known all along that he would break his contract and travel to Key West?

To double check, I asked to see the hotel bill, since I would be paying it. The call John had made was clearly recorded. It was a number I knew well – it was the *Sun*. So how much did they know? Nothing, according to John, who was plainly bullshitting. He could be putting the safety of the team on board the *Nowcani II* in jeopardy. They ought to be in international waters by now but maybe they had been delayed, we just couldn't be sure. John certainly did not know, he had left them at Belem.

There was nothing anyone could do about that now but there would have to be a change of plan. I had intended for them to keep as low a profile as possible, arriving in Barbados at the latest possible time. The idea had been to hand Biggs over to the authorities and let the press hear about it afterwards, now the press would probably be waiting for them!

I had no idea how Jarrett would react. I had called him the previous evening to let him know that Miller had arrived in Key West and, as far as we could tell, the *Nowcani II* was on course for Barbados. One thing was certain: I had to leave for Barbados that same day. From now on, this would be an exercise in crisis management.

On the evening of Thursday March 19th, Veronica Campanile, the former cook of the *Nowcani II*, was stopped by the Belem police, who asked to see her papers. She had been wandering around the town, at a loss for what to do. The money she had taken from Thorfinn Maciver's cabin had nearly run out. She had been snoozing on a chair at a café when the police spotted her, a foreigner without papers.

Because she had jumped ship and left the Belem Yacht Club in a hurry, she had forgotten to have her passport stamped with an entry visa and, because of this, was taken to the local police station for questioning as an illegal immigrant.

Explaining how she had been cook aboard the *Nowcani II*, Veronica went on to tell the police that she had fled the yacht for her own safety. The men on board were British ex-soldiers who had been overheard talking about their plans to kidnap the English train robber, Ronnie Biggs.

The Belem police were not quite sure what to make of this bizarre information and telephoned Rio to check. In fact it was true, the Rio police informed them. Ronnie Biggs was missing! Veronica, who had enough money left for an air ticket, was released on condition she hightailed it to the airport and left Brazil.

In the meantime, the Brazilian authorities had telephoned the Northern Brazil Coastguard, asking them to search for the *Nowcani II* and, in particular, to see if the vessel was still in territorial waters. Next day, a four-engined military patrol aircraft took off from the airfield in Belem, heading for the Atlantic Ocean.

In the early afternoon of March 20th, the team heard the drone of an approaching plane. Fred had allowed Ronnie on deck that day but he was immediately bundled below, protesting loudly. He had been stretched out on deck, enjoying the sun, for all the world as if he had been on holiday. He had to watch from the prison of his cabin, through the portholes, as a large Brazilian military aircraft flew overhead.

Fred stayed with him to make sure he made no attempt to get up on deck and signal the plane, which buzzed them at a really low level, probably about two hundred feet. The side door was open and they could see two members of the aircrew standing there, looking down at them. Thorfinn and Greg waved cheerfully and the plane banked and flew away. If they were looking for someone, they seemed satisfied the object of their search was not on the yacht below, perhaps because it was sailing at a leisurely cruising speed – not for want of urgency to reach their destination but because the generator was still not working properly.

Even though Ronnie had been trapped below, he couldn't resist taunting his captors with what had just happened.

'They've found you now, Fred. I expect they'll be back soon. Or they might just send the coastguard after you.'

'Leave it out, Ron.'

'Look, Fred, the game's up. You might as well face up to it.'

'Face up to what?'

'It's a very serious crime in Brazil, mate. Get you 35 to 50 years. Or you might be shot. Which one do you fancy, Fred?'

'I'll do the time, Ron, then do what you done – escape.'

They both laughed. The plane had gone. Ronnie knew in his heart of hearts it would probably not be coming back again. He switched back to his philosophical mode.

'You do that, Fred. But I hope they shoot that bastard Miller.'

On Thursday March 19th, Adrienne and I, with John and Sarah, all of us posing as holiday-makers, arrived in Barbados at twelve noon, and made our way to the Holiday Inn Hotel. By evening, the world's press was beginning to arrive.

Miller's telephone calls to Britain had alerted the entire media industry. BBC and ITV crews covering the West Indies cricket were diverted from the Test Matches to investigate the rumours flying around in Fleet Street about Biggs' disappearance. The link between what was happening now and the 1979 attempt had suddenly become obvious – otherwise what was Miller doing in Barbados?

Although John was not giving interviews, I guessed he was only biding his time. Also by now we had almost run out of funds. There was nothing for it but to call Jarrett again and ask for a top-up. Due to the time difference between London and Barbados I'd left it too late to get the money required through by telegraphic transfer. I also had to put Jarrett fully in the picture.

Any hopes of the team landing Biggs quietly had been scuppered by John. I accused him of blowing the whole operation. The high point of our adventure should have been the *Nowcani II* sailing into Bridgetown and Biggs being handed over to the authorities – then waiting for the explosion of publicity once back in Britain.

Now it was just going to be uproarious entertainment down at the harbour, a three-ring circus organised by Barnum and Bailey. It seemed to me that Jarrett – since he was the paymaster – would be furious.

We still didn't know, of course, exactly when the *Nowcani II* would arrive. The problem with the generator meant there was no power for radio communication. All we could do was make estimates based on the original plan, which would mean late Sunday or some time Monday. The bitter truth was that the press would probably know before we did. They already had spotter planes out looking for Biggs.

'Listen to this, Pat,' John said. 'I've had a bit of an idea…'

'What?'

'We need to divert the press away from the *Nowcani II*, right?'

'Thanks to you, yes.'

'Well Sarah and I are going to get married, as you know, and so I thought why not here, on Monday?'

Once again John's audacity stunned me. Nothing would deflect the media people from the Biggs story but a wedding could certainly divert their attention for a while.

'You're the craziest bugger I know.'

'You know Jim Davidson's staying on the island? He's always good for a story in the tabloids, famous comedian and all that, usually misbehaving himself…'

'Where does he come into it?'
'He'll be one of the witnesses.'
'Shouldn't you ask him first?'
'I already have. You'll be the other witness, of course.'
'Right,' I said. I had to admit – it was a brilliant idea.

During the third night, the weather turned: it was like a typhoon. The sixty-foot sloop took a battering as it rode high on the waves, only to come crashing down seconds later. During the storm, Biggs, who was in the top bunk, fell out right on top of Fred, who was sleeping below, causing a good deal of startled abuse.

The consequences of the batteries being run down, in their hurry to get away, were now becoming apparent. Because there was no power, the bilge pumps did not work and, as a result, when the *Nowcani II* sprang a leak during the storm, all aboard woke next morning to find themselves up to the waist in water, which needed to be quickly baled out.

Ronnie Biggs states in later accounts that it was he who made the bilge pumps pack up, through the power of positive thinking that he had been practising since Belem, trying to delay the voyage out of Brazil. He also says in telling this particular episode, that he was glad the boat was sinking, his only regret being that Miller was not there to go down with them.

That is not the recollection of Fred Prime and the others who say Ronnie jumped up double quick when the call came for 'All hands on deck' and got stuck in alongside his captors, furiously baling out, using bowls, jugs or whatever they could find.

Thorfinn Maciver, who was as panicked as the rest of them, did manage to isolate the leak and effect a temporary repair. Once they had baled out completely, life on board returned to some kind of normality. The incident, however, had, for big drinkers like Ronnie and Fred, a sobering effect. 'For Those in Peril on the Sea' had never been Ronnie's favourite hymn.

* * *

On the morning of Friday 20th, I called Jarrett in London to let him know exactly what was happening, including John's involvement with the media people.

'I know,' said Jarrett, 'I'm reading about it every day and it's on television too. You realise they'll be hiring planes and fast motor launches, competing to be first to find the *Nowcani II*?'

'Yes,' I replied, 'in that respect it's all gone belly-up. But John has come up with an idea to distract them a bit… He's going to get married.'

There was a moment's silence at the other end and then, surprisingly, a throaty chuckle.

'Good God!'

'He's got it all worked out, there's a famous comedian on the island – it'll be a spectacular show for sure, you can trust John.'

'I'm not sure about the latter but I agree the press will find it entertaining. Now, you wanted money…how much?'

I explained that we did not have enough to cover the Holiday Inn expenses for the four of us, plus I would need money for airfares home for everyone, suggesting a total, and final, payment of another $10,000. Astonishingly, Jarrett agreed without making a fuss.

Then came the problem of getting the money to me in time: just in case there were any legal complications, I did not want to hang around once the job was done. I told Jarrett the best way was for me to send Adrienne over to pick it up in cash. She could then make the return flight.

'I won't be here,' Jarrett said. 'I'm flying to New York this evening. But stick to the plan and I'll give it to your friend, John Howard. Your wife can collect it from him.'

With regard to Biggs' arrival, Jarrett suggested I call John Howard and ask him to contact Scotland Yard, to assure them the rumours they were hearing were true, and allow them to make whatever plans they had in mind to welcome the escaped prisoner. Before ending the conversation, he gave me a number in New York where he could be contacted.

Adrienne flew to London by British Airways that night.

* * *

Another consequence of the power failure was that the satellite navigation equipment was useless, meaning that Thorfinn – the youngest skipper at sea, he claimed – had been obliged to navigate by sextant during the day and by the stars at night.

The others on board – even Fred – were quite confident of the captain's skills and ability to get them to Barbados and so, until Bridgetown came into view, they could relax – or so they thought. Thorfinn gave them an estimated time of arrival as the following Monday, or thereabouts.

The seas were running calm and, apart from having no electricity on board, which meant the lights did not work, they were all very comfortable and in good humour. The worst thing was probably that there was no power to keep the refrigerator running. In the tropical heat the food soon went off and had to be thrown overboard, including some prime cuts of superb Brazilian beef.

The sharks had a good time and followed *Nowcani II* for a couple of days, resulting in much black humour, a lot of it involving Ronnie Biggs. He took it in good part and joined in the banter, giving as good as he got. He seemed resigned to his fate now, whatever that might be. He was convinced that, if he was handed over, he would only serve a few years – and then he would be free, really free for the first time in twenty years in the England he missed so much. He seemed almost glad that the decision had been made for him.

He laughed and joked with the others and could easily be mistaken for a member of the team. He sang along with them and was really cheered when he found a tape of Ravel's 'Bolero', a piece of music he loved.

Tony Marriage began a daily ritual of singing 'The Buccaneer Song' when he was at the helm. It was the theme tune of a British television series called *The Buccaneers* starring Robert Shaw. Each member of the crew, whose turn it was at the helm, would have to start the song, making up verses to suit the day's events and the rest would join in the chorus. The tune was based on the melody of an old folk song but the lyrics left a lot to be desired.

> *Let's go a-rovin', a-rovin' an' join the Buccaneers*
> *Oh Freddie made a stew today,*
> *It was bloody crap,*
> *Ronnie made him walk the plank*
> *To give the sharks a snack*
> *Let's go a-rovin', a-rovin' an' join the Buccaneers.*

Young Greg Nelson loved 'The Buccaneer Song', as did Ronnie who always joined in with gusto. Ronnie also took part in the kitchen chores, claiming he was a better cook than the rest of them put together. One day, while peeling potatoes on deck, he said to Fred:

'Look, Fred, no bullshit... I'll give you a hundred and fifty grand to get me out of this – paid into any bank you like. What do you say?'

'Ronnie, you haven't got two fucking pennies to rub together,' laughed Fred. 'Why don't you give up, mate? I know for a fact you've offered Mark fifty grand and Tony a hundred.'

Fred stayed in good humour but a hint of genuine concern crept into his tone.

'God knows how much you offered Thorfinn,' he said, 'because he's the only one who could get you back to Brazil now and, if he tried it, I'd have to give you both a good smacking. Relax, Ronnie, it'll all be over soon.'

Ronnie liked Fred and knew he meant what he said. They had spent a lot of time talking together and he had told Fred about the train robbers and what had happened when Slipper had tried to arrest him in 1974.

Biggs also got on well with Tony Marriage, but he did not like Mark Algate at all. Mark was nicknamed 'Muscles' because he was a keen bodybuilder and he was always challenging the others to some form of combat. One day, tiring of Mark's boasting, he looked him straight in the eye and took up the challenge.

'All right,' Ronnie told him. 'I'll take you and your tattoos on. Let's have a little wrestle up on deck – All right with you, Fred?' he asked his minder.

'Don't mind me,' said Fred. 'I'm coming up to watch – I hope you know what you're doing Ronnie.'

Algate could not lose face by refusing the challenge and so the bout began, watched by everyone on board. In spite of his age and lack of fitness, Ronnie surprised everyone with his agility, slipping out of Mark's grasp and completely turning the tables on him. He finished up on top of Mark with an arm round his neck, forcing his head back. The others' laughter momentarily turned to real concern as Mark choked:

'Stop him, someone. He's trying to do me...'

Fred stepped in and Ronnie immediately released his hold. Fred pulled him up off his opponent.

'I was only doing what he did to me,' Ronnie excused himself. He obviously had bitter memories of the way he was snatched from the restaurant.

Algate did not take the near defeat well and refused to cooperate with minding Biggs from then on, though he still carried out his sea duties.

Because there was no power, for the last couple of days of the voyage they lived off soup and tinned fruit and, as a result, got upset stomachs. There was also an acute shortage of fresh water: Fred cleaned his teeth using beer instead, although he began to quite like the taste, even first thing in the morning.

And so they sailed on, enjoying the end of their journey on a millionaire's luxury yacht but looking forward to making land again. Because none of the radio-communication gear was working, they had been unable to contact me or John in Bridgetown and so had no idea what kind of reception was waiting for them in Barbados.

They would soon find out.

BARBADOS DEAD AHEAD

When I called John Howard in London to let him know Adrienne was coming over, I also asked him to tip off Scotland Yard, as Jarrett had suggested. Unfortunately, he delegated that responsibility to his colleague Vic Burrill and Burrill, for some reason, decided it would be better to go to Jack Slipper, who obviously had a score to settle with Biggs after having been made to look such a fool when he tried to arrest him in 1974.

Jack Slipper had retired by this time and it took a while to get in contact with him – nothing ever happens fast over an English weekend. It was Monday before Scotland Yard made any kind of official approach to the Barbadian authorities and, by then, a whole train of events had been set in motion.

Over that same weekend, John Miller and I were playing cat and mouse games with the press. I suggested we adopt a three wise monkeys' strategy; that we'd seen nothing, heard nothing and knew nothing. It was a hard one for John to adopt but I was impressed that he seemed to be playing the game. I realised later that this was because John had already sold a so-called exclusive to the tabloids.

An exhausted Adrienne arrived back in Barbados on Sunday evening with the $10,000. Travelling on the same flight was a journalist called Gerry Brown, who was there because his fellow Scotsman, John Miller, had enlisted his help to handle the press. John explained to me that Gerry could be very useful acting as our Press Officer, keeping the press at bay whilst we concentrated in getting Ronnie handed over to the authorities. It was true we were out of our depth trying to handle the large press corps but I wasn't convinced we needed a hack working with us. Personally I believed Brown had been recruited by Miller specifically to sell his own story. Years later, when I worked with Gerry Brown on Central Television's *Cook Report*, my suspicions were confirmed. Miller, Brown told me, had rung, or tried to ring, just about every editor in England and Scotland, maybe even Wales.

The island's bars were packed with tourists and journalists, all discussing Ronald Biggs. Rumours abounded, ranging from the speculative to the downright silly, but John had let enough slip to give the whole world a fair idea of the truth. Biggs had been kidnapped by the same man who had made the headlines eighteen months ago, and was now on his way to Barbados.

Excitement was running high. Not only did they have the arrival of the *Nowcani II* to anticipate but also John Miller's marriage to his beautiful fiancée, Sarah.

Both events were guaranteed to draw in the crowds.

It was late afternoon on Monday March 23rd when those on board the *Nowcani II* heard the sound of a turbo-prop aeroplane. Shielding his eyes against the still bright sun, Tony Marriage was the first to spot the twin-engined Cessna as it buzzed the yacht at about 400 feet. They were approaching Barbados, they knew that, so it was a fair assumption that the plane had taken off from there and that was the only connection they made at first. They still had no radio and not the slightest idea of what had been happening with John and me since we had left Brazil. It did not occur to them that it was the British press searching for them.

Back on the island, John's wedding had turned out to be exactly as he had wanted, with the press corps present in droves. The excited Sarah had picked out a dress from the Holiday Inn boutique, a flouncy linen pastel number, the kind tourists bought when they wanted to dress up for dinner on a tropical island. Adrienne helped her shorten it because the hem fell unfashionably below the petite Sarah's knees. Adrienne then went to the hotel garden and picked some sprigs of bougainvillea for the bride's bouquet.

John, in the meantime, had slipped away silently only to reappear two hours later looking sheepish. He had gone to the local hairdressers to have his hair lightly permed, as was the fashion then, and was spotted by a photographer who promptly snapped a picture of him in curlers. Poor John was mortified at the thought of this image appearing on the front page.

The ceremony itself had been a simple one, with Jim Davidson and me as witnesses. John was at the top of his rollicking form and the only thing that cut short several hours of rowdy celebration was the rumour that *Nowcani II* had been spotted. Although the craft was still some hours away, the guests dispersed rapidly. John's post-nuptials were interrupted by the need for an urgent conference with me on how to manage the event, if there was to be any possibility of doing that in the current chaotic climate. But at least Biggs was in the charge of our men – we assumed – and would be until he was handed over. The truth, we were beginning to realise, was that we were just as much in the dark as to what was happening on board as everyone else.

There was a mounting tension as the yacht drew ever closer to its destination. Everyone was very friendly to Biggs, even Mark Algate, behaving as though they would shortly be losing a buddy. Ronnie himself was philosophical: he had no idea what lay ahead, not in the short term anyway, and, from conversations with Fred, doubted whether his captors had much idea either. He opened a bottle of Grand Marnier and made himself some late lunch. He had been told to stay in his cabin and, his hunger satisfied and with a good book, that suited him. It was not the first time in his life that the future had looked ominous but he was a natural survivor, he knew that.

First of all, there was something he had to do. He was still tremendously concerned about his son and he wanted to make sure, as soon as they had landed in Barbados, that Michael was all right. He asked Fred to post a letter for him when they docked at Bridgetown. Fred agreed only on condition that they both write and sign the letter, in other words he would act as censor. Ronnie consented, reluctantly, and a note was drafted to Armin Heim, asking him to place the boy in Raimunda's care. Still philosophical, he wrote in the letter, 'I'm now actually looking forward to the next move in the game.'

As the sun began to dip in the sky, Mark Algate spotted a fast approaching vessel. Everyone was immediately on alert, standing by for action. As the oncoming craft grew larger, they saw that it was very big indeed, dark grey in colour and bristling with armaments, dwarfing the *Nowcani II* as it drew alongside. Her crew lined the deck, looking down on them. The Barbadian Coastguard had arrived.

'Lower your sails,' ordered the commander through a loud-hailer. 'We are coming aboard.'

'Oh no, you're not!' shouted Fred aggressively. Behind his back, Maciver had already begun to lower sail.

'What do you mean?' demanded the officer, not used to having his commands questioned. 'I must warn you...'

'You are not coming on board,' Fred curtly interrupted him and for the moment there was silence. The commander looked down on the three determined men who confronted him. They were big and burly and, although his crew outnumbered them many times, there was no point in confrontation if it could be avoided. After all, they might also be armed and the skipper, at least, was obeying his instructions.

'Do you have Ronald Biggs on board?' he demanded, taking another tack.

'We're returning a fugitive to justice,' shouted Mark Algate.

'I need to identify him. Bring him on deck!'

Fred was happy to comply with this request. He went to Ronnie's cabin and pulled the somewhat worse-for-wear unfortunate up on deck. Ronnie, wobbling and wearing his sun-hat askew, cut a comic figure.

'What is your name?' shouted the commander.

'Ronnie Biggs,' the man in the funny hat called back, his words slurred, 'and I have been brought here against my will by these bastards…'

Before he could finish his sentence, Fred, Mark and Tony all began laughing and cheering, drowning out his words. Ronnie, who could never take life seriously for long, even in this kind of situation, started laughing back.

'You rotten bastards!' he said, but with more matiness than hostility, and they roared with laughter all the more.

'Take your hat off!' roared the angry Coastguard officer, disconcerted by the amount of frivolity being displayed on board the *Nowcani II*.

Ronnie obediently took his hat off, presumably to aid the officer in identifying him. The whole exercise was completely hilarious as far as he was concerned.

'All right…' shouted the commander and Fred took the hat, jammed it back on Ronnie's head, both men falling about with laughter.

'Let's have another drink,' said Fred.

'You're on, mate.' Suddenly Ronnie began singing:

The sun has got its hat on, hip, hip, hooray,
The sun has got its hat on, all the bastard way…

Both Fred and Ronnie practically tumbled down the steps that led to Ronnie's cabin, their laughter infecting the others. Only the stern commander did not appear to see the funny side. Angrily, he bawled at Maciver:

'We're going to tow you in…'

'We don't need towing in…we can sail in…'

There was no mistaking the determination in the commander's voice.

'No, we are going to tow you in!'

At the same time, one of the crew on board the gunboat threw a rope. It landed at Thorfinn's feet and he, resignedly, took it and tied off at the prow.

The commander nodded, satisfied at last that he had got his way on one thing: the *Nowcani II* was now under escort.

And the man from Rio was on his way to British justice. Perhaps.

A MOST UNUSUAL CASE

Back in Bridgetown, John and I were plotting how to try to regain the initiative, if it were at all possible. Nothing that was happening had been in my plans and John now had to face the consequences of his sabotage.

This was no time for recriminations, however, and I was determined to salvage whatever we could from the operation.

Both of us knew there must be film footage of Biggs on board the *Nowcani II*, since the team had been instructed beforehand to shoot a visual record of Biggs' voyage to show, if necessary, that he had been treated well. This footage had suddenly become very important. Of course, we had no idea of what shots had actually been taken. Depending on what they were, the content could have been quoted as evidence against our team at large and therefore it was vital that the Barbadians did not get hold of it.

John suggested that he should hire a motorised dinghy and race out to the *Nowcani II* in an attempt to secure the film. While this was happening, I would go down to the Coastguard Headquarters in the harbour, waiting for the arrival of the team and their prize.

As the *Nowcani II* approached the harbour, she was met by a whole flotilla of small boats, commandeered for the occasion by the press, including a twenty foot pleasure craft, packed with journalists.

The commander of the gunboat, astonished at their

reception, was genuinely worried that there might be an accident. He ordered the vessel's powerful searchlight to be switched on and its brilliant beam, directed at the *Nowcani II*, lit her up like a Christmas tree.

John, whose dinghy was fast approaching her, immediately changed tack and steered to the dark side of the boat, away from the Coastguards' vessel. The team were all on deck, and the crew: only Ronnie was confined to his cabin. Miller shouted up to Tony Marriage to safe-wrap the film and throw it over. A few minutes later, a large waterproof package, strapped to a lifebelt, was tossed overboard and instantly hauled into the dinghy.

The more astute members of the press, who were keeping an eye on Miller, guided their craft in his wake and, observing the incident, immediately started the rumour that Biggs had been thrown overboard and was drowning. Camera bulbs flashed frantically but no one got a clear picture and John was already speeding back to Bridgetown.

I made my way to the Holiday Inn beach, where Miller landed his craft. Before John could make any kind of excuse, I relieved him of the package. Those photographs were never sold to the newspapers and the film never seen by the public until nearly twenty-five years later in the 2006 British television documentary, *Kidnap Ronnie Biggs*, made for Channel 4.

When the *Nowcani II* docked at the Coastguard jetty in Bridgetown, the darkness was lit by an explosion of flashlights from hundreds of cameras assembled on shore. The scene was like an artillery barrage of the Second World War.

A roar of excitement and relief went up as Ronnie Biggs appeared in the gangway, still wobbly, blinking at the flashlights, his arm held in a vice-like grip by Fred Prime. Fred himself was unsure who he should release his prisoner to among the mob of jostling bodies awaiting them. His dilemma was solved when a man dressed smartly in a naval style uniform – described by Biggs later as having scrambled egg all over the peak of his cap – approached and, with authority, announced himself as the Coastguard commander.

'Hand over the man calling himself Biggs,' he demanded arrogantly.

'No,' said Fred.

'I beg your pardon?'

'Bugger you,' replied Fred, as he brushed past the startled official, still holding tight onto Biggs. 'I haven't come all this way to be messed about by your lot.'

Then, as Fred and Ronnie reached the end of the gangway, they were confronted by a well-dressed Barbadian, who spoke quietly and politely, though with firmness.

'I am Kendrick Hudson,' he said, 'Chief Officer of Immigration. Everyone on board must now go ashore and proceed through Passport Control and Customs. You will be held overnight at the Police Barracks and then released tomorrow morning.' Mr Hudson stood aside to allow the waiting Police Commissioner to take over. Fred then released the prisoner into the Commissioner's custody.

'He's yours now,' Fred said.

'Get in with him.' The Commissioner nodded curtly to the waiting police car, its rear doors open.

'Will I fuck,' replied Fred. 'I've handed him over to the police. That's my job done. I'm going back for a bit of shuteye!' He tried to re-board the *Nowcani II* but his passage was now blocked by various heavyweight police and customs officers, who had taken over the ship.

Hudson went on board to make sure everyone disembarked and the crowd of officers then escorted the Englishmen to the Immigration Office. Kendrick Hudson returned and questioned them about transporting drugs: he too had heard the stories about a package being dumped overboard and this was his take on it. Fred was now tired and growing ever more irritable.

'Do you think we're stupid?' Fred snapped back at him.

'We've got one of the gang who pulled off the biggest robbery of the century and you think we're going to run a bit of marijuana on the side?' Ronnie had of course already smoked all the stuff given to him and there was no evidence left.

Kendrick seemed to see the sense of the argument. This was not the kind of situation he was acquainted with and he was tired too: it was by now three o'clock in the morning. The excitement of the day had all been too much for him. He decided this surly group were not going to be cooperative and handed them over to the police: they could hold them until the proper authorities had time to consider this most unusual, case.

Ronald Arthur Biggs, when he staggered on shore from the *Nowcani II*, was drunk, sleepy and totally disorientated. He was surrounded by a sea of black faces, all gabbling excitedly and following obediently when Kendrick Hudson took possession of the prisoner from Fred Prime.

'Come this way, Mr Biggs,' he was ordered courteously by the Chief of Immigration.

He was taken to a building which he later discovered to be the Bridgetown Police Station and there he was fingerprinted and examined by the police doctor, who announced him to be, not unreasonably, in a state of shock. He was then transferred to accommodation best described as a plainly-furnished room rather than a cell, where he was advised that the British Consul was there to see him if he so wished.

Though feeling shattered, Ronnie did not want to miss the chance of complaining that he had been kidnapped and that he wanted to return to Brazil.

He had what was, from his point of view, a brief but polite conversation with the Consul, to Ronnie's mind the usual kind of upper-class twit associated with Foreign Office diplomats. It was all a bit too much for him to take in after all that had happened but he was assured, following his request, that he would be given the appropriate advice.

'Every British citizen in custody overseas is accorded

consular assistance,' he was told. At the same time, he was not at all sure how seriously this bloke was taking him. He kept burbling on about how he was a representative of Her Majesty's Government and that he had not been instructed…and so on. Ronnie asked if he could see the Brazilian Consul and was told that it was a matter for the Police Chief, and that, for the time being, was how the interview ended.

Gratefully, Ronnie sank on to the bed and, still wondering how the business with the Consul would finish up, fell into a deep, untroubled sleep.

The mysterious package continued to puzzle the customs officers and, the next morning, they arrived at the Holiday Inn to search the rooms occupied by Miller and me. Since they did not know what it was they were looking for, I realised it would be easy to stall them. When they came to search through the luggage, I calmly and deliberately removed my camera equipment and the various rolls of film and laid them all out neatly on the bed for inspection. Singling out a young female officer, I asked her to check over all the gear, emphasising how expensive it was. When the others wanted to question me, I innocently asked the young woman to take charge of the equipment's safe keeping. Baffled and rather embarrassed by the responsibility, the naïve young officer agreed.

Soon after, John and I were taken to Police Headquarters for questioning. Since neither of us had been aboard the *Nowcani II*, there was nothing they could pin on us, particularly as the police had no idea of what we'd been up to in Brazil. After an hour of vigorous but unrewarding questioning, we were released and, taking advantage of where we were, went to visit the others.

Although held in custody overnight, they were all in great spirits. The tiredness of the long, long day before had gone and they were all laughing, not at all dismayed by their incarceration. All three of them, Mark, Tony and Fred, looked fit, tanned and weather-beaten from their voyage. They were all looking forward to their release, however, and the celebrations they were planning to mark the successful accomplishment of their mission.

That afternoon the police, having finished their enquiries, let them go. Although still technically in the charge of the Immigration Department, it was no hard slog since they were sent to stay at Sandy Lane, one of the most exclusive and expensive resorts on the island.

The newspaper and television coverage had of course been enormous. Most of it was inaccurate and speculative. It had certainly not been what John had been expecting since his antics hadn't done anything for his reputation with the press: quite the reverse, the journalists were annoyed with him. On reflection, they had decided that the overall story had much more to offer than the return of wanted criminal Ronnie Biggs, good headline stuff though that might be.

By now the Brazilian government was kicking up a fuss and the press were milking the furious public debate. Was what had happened akin to a successful SAS mission, worthy of medals and a hero's welcome, or were these just a bunch of money-grubbing mercenaries who had kidnapped a reformed criminal, leading an honest and law-abiding life in Rio de Janeiro until wrenched away from his wife and baby son? Some tabloids dared to suggest that Biggs was no longer the vicious and violent criminal they had always portrayed but a plucky underdog! No praise was forthcoming for attempting to return a fugitive to justice.

There was no doubt about how the Brazilian authorities were taking the matter and, on the Wednesday, we learned they were seeking extradition orders against John and me. I telephoned Jarrett giving him an account of the situation. He indicated that nothing would happen to us as far as the extradition was concerned, but advised leaving the island as soon as possible. Clearly, it was time for us to take our leave of Barbados.

John and his wife left as soon as they could, returning home. It was a somewhat subdued John Miller who set foot on British soil again. There was no glory, just frustration and embarrassment. The press were down on him. Like many before him, he was discovering the disadvantages of being in the public eye. The man who had married the glamorous daughter of a rich merchant banker in a glitzy ceremony in Barbados was now reported as someone who had been falsely claiming social security benefits. There was also a warrant out for his arrest, laid by English magistrates for failing to appear in court to answer previously laid charges of common assault in a nightclub, involving pop musician Denny Lane of Paul McCartney's band Wings.

Adrienne and I took the last flight out on Wednesday night, to the neighbouring island of Trinidad, and flew to Puerto Rico on Thursday morning. Fred, Tony and Mark also left Bridgetown on the Thursday flying direct to London.

Thorfinn Maciver and Greg Nelson were freed and remained in Barbados. Thorfinn had claimed to the authorities that he was a victim of the gang and forced to cooperate for fear of his life – although strangely no action was ever taken against the kidnappers in respect of this claim. As captain of the *Nowcani II*, he had to remain anyway until the boat was released by Customs. They had searched every nook and cranny of *Nowcani II*, to his dismay, causing him to complain that they had done $10,000* worth of damage, but no claim was ever made against them.

These events marked the end of our adventure to kidnap Ronnie Biggs, still held in captivity pending extradition proceedings. The Biggs' saga was not yet ended, however. The drama was still to come.

* worth $40,000 today

THE THIEF IS OURS

David Montgomery was the United Kingdom's Deputy High Commissioner for the Eastern Caribbean stationed in Barbados where, among other duties, he was responsible for consular matters.

It was not a particularly taxing position. Barbados is English-speaking and much of the local scene was familiar to anyone from Britain. The island depended on tourists of course, but the hotel management were highly skilled at dealing with most of the minor problems that arose. There was the usual quota of nationals in trouble, lost passports, lost money, the very occasional theft of possessions but nothing on the scale of what he was about to encounter.

He was having dinner at the High Commissioner's residence when a telephone call was received late in the evening from the local police saying that a yacht had been identified, approaching the island, with someone apparently on board called Ronnie Biggs. Montgomery remembered the name, the Great Train Robbery and the subsequent escape but, as he says, had not really thought about him since.

Intrigued, he asked to be kept informed and stayed up late, until the early hours of the morning, when he was advised by Orville Durant, the Deputy Commissioner of Police, that the yacht was now approaching the harbour, and asked if he would like to accompany Durant to the dockside, to greet the unwelcome visitor.

At the harbour, he watched with astonishment as the *Nowcani II* drew in, and, in due course, disgorged its notorious passenger. There was a tremendous crowd, many of them press. Montgomery had no idea there were so many journalists on the island – how did they know this man Biggs was on board the broken-down yacht? He was amazed at the incredible scrimmage that ensued when Mr Hudson, the Chief of Immigration, took charge of the prisoner. Everyone was pushing and shoving and shouting out questions to Biggs, principally wanting to know if he had been knocked about at all – an irrelevance in Montgomery's eyes. So far as he could see, Biggs looked fit and well, somewhat dazed perhaps at his reception, not surprisingly, or possibly he was somewhat intoxicated.

He watched Biggs being pushed into a police car and then followed the small convoy of vehicles to the police station, where, in due course, he was introduced to the great train robber. Commenting on the event in the 2005 Channel 4 documentary, *Kidnap Ronnie Biggs*, he found Mr Biggs, somewhat to his surprise, composed and articulate, though wary.

The prisoner immediately complained that he had been brought to the island against his will and wanted to be returned to his family in Brazil as soon as possible.

This was not an unexpected request of course, but Montgomery politely informed Biggs that, while he fully understood the other's position, Her Majesty's Government might well take another view of the matter.

In fact, he said, warming to his task, he thought it was undoubtedly the case that the British Government would seek his extradition to the United Kingdom to resume the sentence that had been regrettably interrupted. And with that he bade the prisoner a courteous goodnight, though he could not resist a parting shot:

'See you in court, Mr Biggs.'

* * *

No one disturbed Ronnie as he slept on till late morning. When he awoke he found himself in a strange room furnished with a single bed and a table and chair, where a stout black man sat reading a newspaper. At first he was not sure if he was still dreaming but then the shooting pain of a massive hangover convinced him that this was reality and kaleidoscopic images of the events from the previous night flooded back into his head.

'Good morning,' he ventured.

The fat black man lowered his paper. 'Good morning, sir,' he said.

This was encouraging. 'Any chance of a wash and brush-up?' he asked.

The man escorted him to the lavatory and left him alone to complete his ablutions. When Ronnie came out the man was waiting to take him back to his cell, where a breakfast of coffee and croissants had been brought in for him.

He had hardly finished breakfast when he was paid a visit by Kendrick Hudson again, who asked how he was and whether he had spent a comfortable night. Ronnie was beginning to warm to the courteous islanders of Barbados. Hudson went on to explain that Biggs' presence in the police station was because he had entered Barbados without a passport – a very minor offence in his book – and that in due course he would be placed in the charge of Immigration where he would be allowed more comfortable quarters until the matter had been cleared up.

Ronnie was by now cheering up considerably: no one had mentioned the train robbery or, apart from the British Consul in passing, the matter of extradition. His kidnappers, it appeared, were also in custody in this same police station. Never a man to see a half-full glass as a half-empty one, his spirits began to rise. Would it be possible to pull off a Houdini escape again?

This view was tempered somewhat when he met later with Mr Whittaker, the Chief of Police. Coppers are coppers, Ronnie realised with sinking heart again, of any colour and in any language. Whittaker knew he was the wanted train robber all right and the policeman left him in no doubt that he wanted to see him returned to the UK.

He was not impressed when Ronnie began to bluster that he was the victim in this instance, who wanted repatriation to Brazil immediately and his captors to be severely punished. Whittaker shrugged and said he was not aware of any criminal intent on their part and, so far as he was concerned, they could be released as soon as he had completed his enquiries. The only criminal act that had taken place, it seemed, was Mr Biggs – even if not of his own volition – landing on the island without a passport.

No sooner had Ronnie returned to his room, than yet another visitor was announced, a Mr Ezra Alleyn. They certainly allowed plenty of visits in this nick, thought Ronnie. Who the hell was this one, when he was at home?

When the man entered, he said nothing, just stood in the doorway and smiled. He looked somehow familiar and, after staring at him for a few moments, baffled at the visitor's enigmatic smile, the penny dropped for him.

'Sunshine!' he yelled. 'Is that you?'

Ezra Alleyn was a native of Barbados, a bespectacled lawyer. Unlike the previous visitor, he knew Ronnie Biggs well, having been a junior clerk in the court at Aylesbury Assizes. He had been studying in London at the time of the Great Train Robbery, under the tutelage in fact of Ellis Lincoln, the solicitor who had handled the defences of great train robbers Hussey, Welch and Wisbey at the trial. He remembered chatting with Biggs, who, because he came from Barbados, always called him 'Sunshine'.

He had come to offer his services, he said, and presented a pitch that was hugely impressive, especially since he claimed he had never lost a case.

'I am known on the island,' he added modestly, 'as the Perry Mason of Barbados.'

A Perry Mason – the fictional American television attorney who never lost a case – was more than enough for Ronnie Biggs, although he had to admit that he had no money to pay for his defence, a protestation that was brushed aside by Mr Alleyn. It seemed as though he was quite prepared to represent Ronnie without any money up front, perhaps shrewdly guessing that elements of the world's press would be queuing up to pay the costs. He had sat through the original trial of the train robbers and had followed their respective careers with interest ever since, especially Ronnie Biggs. He knew the huge amount of publicity this case would generate and had no doubt his fees would be more than adequately recouped. It was a genuine offer, however, and he radiated optimism.

'There is always a loophole, Mr Biggs,' he said. 'I was taught that by Mr Lincoln. We will find a loophole and you will be sent back to Brazil, not the UK.'

Ronnie's spirits rose again. He had a brief now, for free, and Perry Mason into the bargain. He shook hands warmly with his would-be saviour and gratefully accepted the offer.

But events were to take yet another turn.

While Jarrett, in New York, was receiving a telephone call from me reporting on events so far, and arranging a meeting for later in the week, there was a flurry of activity on the other side of town.

David Neufeld, an American attorney of some repute, was also taking a telephone call from England. The caller was David Levy, the author of a book – with Ronnie Biggs – entitled *Ronnie Biggs: His Own Story*. Serialisation rights had been sold to the *Sun* newspaper and the editor must have been thanking his lucky stars with all this brouhaha going on worldwide at the same time as they were running the series of articles.

Neufeld was aware of the stories on the TV news and in the papers but the name Ronnie Biggs was not really meaningful to him. However, the case as outlined by Levy certainly sounded intriguing and there was no problem about his fees being met, he was assured. With Levy offering to pay all costs and with the book's publishers and the *Sun* in the background, he felt quite certain there would be no problems financially. He accepted the case and made preparations to fly to Bridgetown.

If he had not known who Ronnie Biggs was before, Neufeld was certainly aware of his new client's identity by the time he got to the airport – even the American newspapers were beginning to headline the story: to do so about a British criminal was little short of sensational. Arriving in Bridgetown, he could see the whole town was in the grip of Biggs mania. Taxi drivers, bartenders, just about everyone, seemed to have no other topic of conversation and he was surprised to find how much sentimental support there was for the man who was undoubtedly a notorious criminal but who had, it appeared, been living a law-abiding existence in Rio de Janeiro with a wife and baby son.

He was feeling confident by the time he got to his hotel, unpacked, showered and changed, and prepared to meet his client.

Ronnie Biggs in Bridgetown gaol was quite unaware that he was about to be given a new lawyer.

What would happen to Perry Mason?

Ronnie Biggs had no idea just how many people were on his side. Romeo Zero, the Brazilian Consul, who had been in office for only two weeks, was also caught up in this tangled web of events. What he had assumed would be a peaceful and relaxing assignment in Barbados had all the makings, he could see, if not handled properly, of a massive diplomatic crisis.

Romeo did of course know who Ronnie Biggs was and, when the *Nowcani II* had docked at Bridgetown and Biggs was taken into custody, he had gone to the gaol to find out what was happening. There, he was told they were detaining a man who claimed to be Biggs but, because he had no documents on his person, they could not be sure of that at the present time.

He did not attempt to gain access to Biggs at this stage. So far as he was concerned, this was a diplomatic matter involving three countries, Brazil, Barbados and the UK – if indeed the man was Biggs – and would have to be settled by negotiation, behind the scenes.

Returning to his consulate, he made enquiries in Brasilia and Rio de Janeiro, where he found there was now a definite assumption that Biggs had been kidnapped. On application to the Barbadian foreign ministry he was told that, nevertheless, there was no extradition agreement between the island and Brazil, and Biggs could not be returned as yet, indeed if at all. He was informed that Biggs was now the subject of a United Kingdom extradition application.

Romeo continued to receive instructions from Brasilia where, despite there not being an extradition treaty between Brazil and Barbados, they still felt entitled to demand the extradition of the kidnappers, if not Biggs.

Those prisoners had, in fact, already been released by the Barbadian authorities and were celebrating the success of the feat at a first-class hotel while waiting to catch a flight back home. This was to the dismay of Sergeant Ellison, an officer who had been sent with a colleague to Barbados by Scotland Yard.

The policemen had been met by David Montgomery, and Ellison had made no attempt to hide the animosity he felt towards the kidnappers, especially John Miller, probably because they had succeeded in getting Biggs, where the Yard had failed.

Ellison disliked the kidnap team and had been desperate to find a charge that would stick against Miller and company, but the best he could come up with was piracy on the high seas! Eventually he was told by his bosses at the Yard that they had been informed by their superiors to leave the team alone. There would be no further pursuit of anyone involved.

Romeo Zero was aware of Scotland Yard's presence on the island but chose to ignore it, remaining the quintessential diplomat, polite but forceful, not getting involved with Biggs while expressing clearly the concern of his own country, which was that on their territory a man had been abducted by foreign nationals. This was a matter of sovereignty, not because they had any special regard for Ronnie Biggs. Romeo summed up their arguments succinctly:

'In this case, the thief is ours.'

A VERY BRITISH COUP

Ronnie Biggs, insofar as the circumstances allowed, was enjoying himself. He was annoyed to learn that his British kidnappers had been released but the kindly Fred Prime had taken the trouble to leave $100* at the gaol for Ronnie's day to day expenses.

He breakfasted in bed, reading a newspaper, ordered flying fish or some other delicacy for lunch, was visited every day by the police chief, Whittaker, or Mr Hudson, who had now taken charge of the prisoner. Ronnie was resident in a block which housed some twenty immigration officers, all of whom had queued up to get his autograph when he arrived.

David Neufeld had been something else, quite different from Ezra Alleyn, a razor-sharp, beautifully dressed, slick Manhattan lawyer, who claimed he had been instructed by David Levy, the author of Ronnie's book. Though surprised, Ronnie was still very glad to see him. At the same time, he was reluctant to part with the services of Ezra Alleyn, and he said so.

Neufeld was dismissive of Alleyn at first. He had done his homework and learned that the best lawyer on the island was Frederick Smith QC and, as far as he was concerned, he was here in Barbados to secure Smith's services and he did not expect any argument to the contrary from his client.

Ronnie, for all his faults, was a loyal person. He had taken a liking to Ezra and they had this kind of shared bond arising

* worth $400 today.

from the coincidence of the link to the original trial. He had also found out that the proposed counsel was known as Frederick 'Sleepy' Smith, which did not much appeal to him. In fact, 'Sleepy' Smith was anything but, his nickname being due to a 'lazy eye', and, in the course of time, would become Sir Frederick Smith, Lord Chief Justice.

In the end, a compromise was agreed. Although Neufeld grumbled, Frederick Smith QC and Ezra Alleyn, together with a rising young lawyer named Shepherd, would work as a team representing Biggs, who thus got the three best lawyers on the island pleading his case, at absolutely no expense to himself.

Neufeld's instructions to the team of barristers was crystal clear and quite straightforward. His client had been eating at a restaurant when he was attacked, kidnapped, forcibly bound and removed from his own country. He was then taken to a neutral country before his final intended destination. The mission, in the view of his abductors, had been accomplished and Barbados was no more than a weigh station before Biggs was sent back to England.

This, Neufeld said, was a grotesquely arrogant assumption. The people who should be in prison were the kidnappers who, in fact, had been freed from custody and allowed to return home. In his opinion, the operation must have had the backing of the British Government and he felt that this was where they had to make a stand. A government had decided to grab someone on foreign soil and this was what they had done. It was a situation of international intrigue.

By now, the hearing had been set for April 5th, giving the team only a few days to prepare a vigorous defence.

Before long, Ronald Biggs would learn his fate.

That fate was of interest not only to Biggs but also to the general public worldwide. A debate raged as to whether, in effect, he was some kind of Robin Hood figure – at least Robin of Sherwood robbed the rich to give to the poor, the train robbers just robbed the ordinary people to keep it themselves! Was Biggs worthy of rehabilitation, or a violent criminal who had cocked a snook at the law, and got away with it for too long. Did he thoroughly deserve to be returned to the gaol he had escaped from, to serve out the rest of his sentence? This debate was to surface again many years later.

David Montgomery, the British Deputy High Commissioner to the Eastern Caribbean in 1981, poses an interesting theory: that all communities have two populations, the middle and upper classes who form the establishment, and an underclass which, though not criminal in itself, will always side with one of its own.

This was his description of Ronnie Biggs as stated in 2005:

'I can't say I warmed to Ronnie Biggs. I saw him as I had probably imagined, a fairly typical petty criminal. He struck me as being oblivious to the feelings of others. Someone who was fairly self-centred, who had chosen a path in life which necessitated him being inevitably wary, always defensive, invariably very guarded in conversation with whoever he was speaking to, unless it was someone that he knew as an accomplice, so to speak. But no, I would not say that he was the sort of person I would choose to share a single malt with. No.'

By now the Brazilian media were becoming hysterical about the affront to their sovereignty. An international crisis was looming. All believed there was official British government involvement behind the abduction. 'AN OUTRAGE' screamed the headlines.

Seven-year-old Michael Biggs was televised appealing to the British government. His angelic face pleaded to the camera:

'I know the Queen wants my father in prison but I need my father more.'

It was emotional stuff. No news editor could have asked for better. The wife of the Brazilian Foreign Minister was so overcome by the broadcast that she rang the most powerful wives in the country telling them to insist their husbands do everything in their power to reunite Michael with his poor father. It was of course the ultimate irony. Here was one of the most powerful women in Brazil wanting to be seen as saving the country's honour on the one hand but who, in our opinion, did little to help the plight of Brazil's street children who were being reportedly murdered at the rate of thirty a week by the country's own police force.

On Sunday March 29th, I met with Jarrett in New York. Towards the end of our chat about the whole operation, I told him how Barbadian customs had caused $10,000 worth of damage to the yacht during their detailed searches and that Maciver had asked me to help; also that the American owner had threatened to sue Miller.

'We don't want to leave any loose ends,' Jarrett said thoughtfully. 'We'll pay the damages. I'll get the money to you on your return to London.'

Then, after a long pause, he said, 'By the way, pay Maciver through your lawyer just to make sure the Texan owner gets the money. We don't want it to end up in Maciver's pocket, if you know what I mean.'

Jarrett's instructions surprised me. Why pay Maciver anything, I thought? Again, Jarrett's actions only confirmed my belief that there was official backing. They wanted no loose ends left, otherwise why pay?

To my surprise, since Jarrett had been quite snappy once or twice about the amount of money being spent, there was no argument and the extra money would be found. Moreover, unlike me, Jarrett seemed to be quite pleased with the outcome of the venture we had planned together, what seemed like years ago but in fact was only five months since.

We talked about the coming court case in Barbados, naturally, but Jarrett was more inclined to listen to what views I put forward than to express his own, other than to hint, somewhat mysteriously, that I shouldn't be surprised if events didn't turn out the way I expected.

The meeting ended with Jarrett telling me to call him on the same New York number in two weeks' time.

It was now just a matter of tying up the loose ends before returning back to London.

PART FOUR

What happened after…

THE TRIAL (1)

There were three hearings in all before the Ronnie Biggs case was concluded. The first of these concerned a writ of *Habeus Corpus* which had been issued by Frederick Smith as an opening ploy in the game. This was delivered somewhat tongue-in-cheek by Smith who, though leading defence counsel, quite understood why the British establishment, who had been mocked by him for eighteen years, would want Biggs back.

He had seen Biggs pictured on a billboard advertising men's Y-fronts with the brash slogan: *When you're on the run like me, you need the freedom of briefs like these.* No wonder he got under their skin.

David Neufeld's first day in court proved to be an eventful one. Sitting with the defence team, watching Biggs in the dock, he was gripped by the arm by a burly official and asked whether he had work papers which allowed him to practise in a Barbadian court. He had no such documentation of course and his irritable protests went unheard. He was told that he was leaving and was physically escorted from the building. The application for *Habeus Corpus* failed.

Even today, Neufeld is convinced that the official was acting on the direction of a higher authority. True, the direct intervention was that of the Barbadian Government but who was pulling the strings? At the time, he had no doubt that the orders were being issued by the United Kingdom.

The incensed Neufeld went straight to the US Embassy to complain but they refused to get involved. He decided to regularise his situation: by flying to New York and then returning the same day by another aircraft, this time as an ordinary tourist and not as a lawyer.

His plan now was to invoke the international Human Rights Treaty, claiming Ronald Biggs' rights had been violated, while leaving the local defence team to concentrate on matters affecting the laws of Barbados. What struck Neufeld as being particularly suspicious was that every time he mentioned the kidnapping, no one denied it but just asked for proof. How else had Biggs arrived on the island and why had his abductors been allowed to return to the UK? Again the answer was always that their papers had been in order and there had been no reason to detain them since no crime had been committed on Barbadian soil.

Neufeld knew he had to continue making trouble for the authorities, even though he knew he had no legal status there. The next hearing would deal with the application for extradition and he wanted to block that by raising the question of the kidnapping. His job was to get Ronnie Biggs back to Brazil and he did not care how many feathers he ruffled. He tried to play one side against the other, claiming this was an affront to the Brazilian authorities even though they appeared to want to conduct the negotiations in a low key. There had been no direct contact between the British and Brazilian governments and both were appearing to want to leave the matter to the Barbadians, while the Barbadian government was definitely uncomfortable in the hot seat.

In opposing bail for Biggs at the start of the extradition hearing, Eliot Belgrave, who led the prosecution, claimed that if the application was granted, the prisoner would immediately make a beeline for the Brazilian Diplomatic Mission, from where it would be impossible to extract him. When this was put to Ronnie, he was quite shocked, claiming that such an idea had never even entered his head.

The magistrate, Mr Frank King, was unmoved by this heartfelt declaration and Ronnie was obliged to stay locked up during the hearing. This began with Whittaker, the police chief, giving evidence describing Biggs' arrival on the island, making it clear that his department wanted the prisoner returned to Britain.

Frederick Smith, who had been the Attorney General at the time of Independence and was the senior counsel on the island, declared in his booming and authoritative voice that the poor man had been kidnapped off the streets of Rio de Janeiro and should be returned there immediately.

There was the usual argument about whether the extradition request was in order. The defence claimed it was not, since one of the related orders had not been approved but this was taken as the usual nit-picking and, after adjourning the Court to allow the police to present any relevant documents, the magistrate decided he was satisfied that the request had been made properly and should be granted, though he gave Biggs leave to appeal.

So far it had all gone very much as anticipated. David Montgomery had said that the British Government expected the Barbadians to play a straight bat and, as befitted a cricketing nation, they had done exactly that.

The first innings does not always decide a match, however. The second innings was still to come.

THE TRIAL (2)

Romeo Zero, the Brazilian Consul to Barbados, though keeping diplomatically away from the action, was keeping a keen eye on the hearing. More and more people had been arriving in the square by the court, every day, ever since Biggs had been deposited in Bridgetown.

There was a fever of speculation among the population about the possible outcome of the court proceedings and the government was getting distinctly worried. A general election was due fairly shortly and the government felt that if the result was unfavourable – that is to Biggs – then it might affect the result. They were most concerned about the way people were reacting to Ronnie Biggs' being imprisoned. Every day saw larger crowds gathering outside the court to show their sympathy for the prisoner in his plight, and to support his battle against authority.

Using a go-between, Tom Adams, the Prime Minister of Barbados, enquired of Romeo what would happen if Biggs were to be released – would they be prepared to take him off the island and back to Brazil? And if it were possible, given that Biggs had no papers of any kind, could it be done quickly and privately, and before anyone could react?

Romeo was intrigued and couched his reply in moderate terms. The Brazilian Government had no special interest in Biggs other than the fact that he had been forcibly removed from their jurisdiction. Both Brazil and the UK had taken care not to discuss the matter directly, always referring the matter to Barbados, who could not please both sides. The fiction of this being a strictly legal matter was beginning to be exposed. Romeo was in daily touch with Brasilia and his superiors there had told him there was a definite unease between the UK and Barbados: they had perceived a real tension developing.

It was clear to Romeo, at least, that Biggs' release was going to be a political decision rather than a legal one. Neither Brazil not the UK wanted to see this matter escalate into a diplomatic crisis and both were looking to Barbados for a face saving solution.

David Montgomery's theory about the underclass may have been borne out by the gathering crowds chanting Biggs' name. What he had perhaps overlooked was that the underclass also had massive voting power and that a general election was due.

How could the Government of Barbados resolve its own internal crisis?

On April 7th, I received the money from Jarrett as promised and paid Thorfinn Maciver, who had flown to London, $10,000* in respect of all claims arising out of the charter of the *Nowcani II* from its millionaire owner, Robert Sabinske, Maciver's principal.

The job was finished, everyone paid. We had gone over budget but for reasons beyond our control. Anyway, the client had seemed satisfied, although, admittedly, I had never been really sure what was going on in Jarrett's head, what it was he really wanted or what he truly wanted to accomplish. Was Jarrett himself a pawn, an agent of Her Majesty's Government? I asked myself again. Or even of some other government?

John Miller, in the meantime, was having no luck selling his own story about the kidnap, which was not surprising since he had given most of the information away for free. He sold a photo to the *Sunday Mirror* of the snatch, depicting himself hauling the bag with Ronnie inside into the van. But the photo

* worth $40,000 today

was a fake! The man inside the bag was actually Fred Prime pretending to be Biggs. John had persuaded Fred to participate in the photo, taken by Thorfinn Maciver while he was in London, for fun so they could send it to their army mates. The *Sunday Mirror* withdrew the picture after one edition.

Of course, in a way it was not really over at all, not yet, assuming that the intention had been to put Biggs behind bars again. Ronnie seemed to be playing a blinder out in Barbados, and public opinion, on the whole, was firmly on his side. The villains in the drama, mainly due to John Miller's antics, had definitely been us: we were denigrated in every possible way by the press, portrayed as money-grubbing bounty hunters. The quote I like the best was 'More like Laurel and Hardy than Dogs of War'.

I don't believe the bad feeling against us would have existed if the original plan, to disappear quietly after handing Biggs over, had been implemented. The media, of course, knew nothing of Jarrett, nor did they know about his superiors. Kidnapping Ronnie had been the perfect 'deniable operation'.

Soon, the final act of this particular drama would be played out, when the Barbadian Lord Chief Justice heard Ronnie Biggs' appeal. Whether he would be returned to Brazil or extradited to the UK was a decision no longer in our hands.

Ronnie Biggs' life story might be an ongoing adventure but, so far as I and the others were concerned, we were no longer a part of it. Our job had been done: it made no difference now whether Ronnie was returned to Brazil or not. Though a charming rogue to all who met him, behind the façade was still a petty crook who had, by chance, been present at a big pay day. He possessed the cunning that allowed him to escape and make fools of the police for nearly twenty years.

Except, of course, with Biggs, you just never know…

Following the first hearing, Ronnie received some sad news. He would no longer be in the charge of the Immigration Office, the kindly Mr Hudson told him, but the police. Mr

Whittaker, Ronnie knew, was a very different cup of tea.

Gone were his comfortable quarters, to be replaced by a dark cell, infested with cockroaches, in Glendairy Prison. The normally cheerful train robber was in despair again as he heard the clang of the heavy front gates close behind him and he was subjected to the routine he knew so well. The 'screws' were similar to British warders but more strict, very regimented. One of them would have served as a model for Mr McKay, the warder in the British TV series *Porridge*, with his thin pencil moustache and swagger stick.

He was asked his name – as if no one knew who he was! – and his practically non-existent personal property was recorded in a large tome. Passing through more locked iron gates, opened for him with the usual prison routine jargon, he was shown to Cell 10. It had a cot with a lumpy mattress and an evil-smelling commode in one corner. The door was of steel mesh rather than bars and he was able to chat through it with the prisoners in other cells, which were either side of a corridor, at the end of which was a forbidding black door.

Biggs gives what is a dramatic but probably highly fanciful account of his time in 'Death Row', as he calls it. Some of his fellow-prisoners were, he says, waiting for *de rope* and the black door.

David Montgomery, the British Deputy High Commissioner, derides this account however, claiming that there is and was no capital punishment on the island, certainly not during Biggs' stay.

Death penalty or not, the conditions were unappealing, even for one so familiar with the inside of prisons. His case was still a *cause celebre* though, and every day he received masses of mail from well-wishers. Never down for long in his belief in the power of positive thinking, Ronnie just prayed that his lucky star, which had been with him so long, had not dimmed and would be shining down on him come the day of the appeal.

He did not have long to wait. All parties desperately wanted a solution to the problem that was Ronnie Biggs, while realising that their own wishes were incompatible. Great Britain had no desire to challenge Brazil's sovereignty. Brazil did not want to be seen as a country harbouring a criminal and Barbados was the piggy in the middle.

But what was the answer?

THE GREATEST ESCAPE

At the time of Barbadian independence, 30th November 1966, extradition was covered by what was known as the *Fugitive Offences Act* of 1887. All independent countries like to make their own legislative amendments and these were put into force in 1971. The new legislation was very similar to its predecessor, since it was based on it.

The legislation that covered extradition, because it followed the previous act, was called 'an act of continuation', a procedure which does not have to be debated in parliament. It is drafted, submitted to the Governor General for Royal Assent and, when given, the substantive orders of the act are placed before parliament for a period of forty days, after which it is confirmed law.

The Act not having been placed before Parliament for forty days was the legal point on which Frederick Smith and his defence team relied when appearing before the Chief Justice, Sir William Douglas, there to hear the appeal against Biggs' extradition.

Prosecuting Counsel Eliott Belgrave disagreed. He argued the Extradition Act gave the power to the appropriate minister to make an order. A ministerial order had to be made, signed and proclaimed, and that was all there was to it. To invalidate the new act would require a negative vote in Parliament and, until that was done, the treaty was valid.

Belgrave still believes to this day that the treaty was valid enough for Biggs to be returned to Britain. Political expediency had crept into the affair and public opinion also favoured Biggs. The loophole was a convenient one.

The crowd outside the court was enormous and consisted mostly of well-wishers for Biggs. They shouted encouragement as he was brought from the gaol and a stout black lady in a flowery hat, who had turned up every day since the first hearing, was there to bless him. She was praying for him constantly, she called out.

The courtroom was also packed with many friendly faces, including David Levy, who had arranged for Biggs' defence, and Ronnie's old friend from Rio, Armin Heim, the photographer. The lawyers, Frederick Smith and Ezra Alleyn, murmured words of encouragement to the prisoner and told him they were confident of their grounds, though Ronnie was not too sure what they were – it had been explained to him but was too legal and technical for him to grasp.

Whittaker, the Police Chief, standing by Biggs in the dock, also looked confident. The Clerk of the Court said whatever it was he had to say, all rhubarb as far as Ronnie was concerned, and then Frederick Smith rose to put the case for the appeal.

Smith and his team had done their homework well. They touched on the validity of the extradition proceedings at the earlier hearing, which had been given short shrift by the magistrate, but now there were more substantive points to be made.

There had been an administrative lapse, he claimed, and the orders of the 1971 Extradition Act had not been placed before Parliament for forty days as they should have been. Moreover, unless these acts of continuation had been challenged during the forty days, they became law – but if they had not been there to challenge, there had been no opportunity for them to become law.

It was all way over Ronnie Biggs' head and probably just as incomprehensible to the rest of the bodies in the court, but Sir William Douglas seemed to take it seriously and retired to consider the point.

There was a general hubbub when he did so, with everyone trying to work out what it meant, including Biggs. Smith came over to the dock to reassure him, telling him it was a technicality but a very important one and the longer it was being considered, the better it was for the prisoner.

Ronnie, heart in mouth, waited as the minutes ticked by. After about a quarter of an hour, the loud and fevered speculation in the court died to a more respectful murmur as they all stood for the re-entry of the Chief Justice.

The tension in the court was unbearable. The press and TV were there in force, including Romeo Zero's son, who was a cameraman for Globo, the giant Brazilian broadcasting company. In the strict silence observed while everyone listened to the judge, only the sound of mass breathing could be heard.

His ruling was short and to the point. It was imperative, said the Chief Justice, that the laws of the island should be observed to the letter and proper procedures, as laid down in law, must be followed, also to the letter in all cases. He agreed with Mr Smith's contention that the necessary procedures in this case were not properly followed and therefore he allowed the appeal. Mr Biggs was free to leave the court.

There was a moment's stunned silence and then utter pandemonium broke out. David Levy rushed to the dock and had to convince the overwhelmed Ronnie that he really could walk out of the court without hindrance and as a free man.

David Levy and David Neufeld escorted Biggs out to the waiting, cheering crowds. The black woman who had prayed for his release was in floods of tears and waited to kiss him. Everyone wanted to shake Ronnie's hand or pat him on the back.

Romeo Zero was waiting in a hired taxi and Biggs was pushed into the back, momentarily fearful because he had no idea who Romeo Zero was. Neufeld, ever cautious, still mistrusted the British Government and insisted on getting Ronnie back to Brazil as quickly as possible. He arranged for a jet to fly in from Miami to transport them to Belem that night.

Biggs was taken to the Brazilian Diplomatic Mission just outside Bridgetown where he kissed the portrait of the Brazilian president hanging in the corridor. Romeo Zero shortcut all the usual procedures to get him on his way. Since he had no documents of identity, he was issued by Romeo with a safe conduct. The necessary photograph was obtained by photocopying the likeness on the back of David Levy's book.

The legal loophole, as promised by Ezra Alleyn, had been found. Both the British and the Brazilian governments had passed the buck to the islanders, saying they could not interfere with the Barbadian legal system. The Barbadians had responded in the best traditions of British justice, by finding a compromise in their own unfortunate – or fortunate – neglect of detail.

Ronnie flew back to be reunited with his son in Rio that same night.

But even in this hour of triumph, controversy surrounded Ronnie Biggs. It was to do with the Lear Jet that flew him back to Brazil and freedom. Although it was Neufeld who had arranged for the plane, he did not pay the $18,000 hire charge. David Levy had said he would pay and then recoup the amount by charging the Brazilian and Australian television journalists accompanying the flight.

According to Sir Frederick Smith QC, who had been the leading defence barrister, he was asked to fund the $18,000 as a temporary loan, so there would be no delay in getting Biggs out. 'Sleepy' Smith duly obliged but was never repaid. The television companies paid up their shares but no one knows who got the money. Sleepy, annoyed, sent several written requests for the money to Biggs in Rio but never received a penny.

A few years later, when appointed Lord Chief Justice of Barbados, Sir Frederick Smith QC was invited to meet Her Majesty Queen Elizabeth II of England and Barbados at a reception on board the Royal Yacht *Britannia*. On being introduced to Prince Phillip, he was asked if he was the same Frederick Smith who had defended the fugitive Ronnie Biggs?

'I am,' replied Sir Frederick, 'and furthermore he still owes me $18,000 for the jet that was hired to take him back to Brazil.'

'Serves you right,' said the Duke of Edinburgh, 'for defending a damn train robber.'

THE END...?

PART FIVE

Where are they now…?

POSTCRIPT

The end of the Biggs affair is as strange as its beginning. It was considered by many to be one of the most bizarre capers of the1980s and affected the lives of many people. Like all affairs it had its winners and its losers.

Ronnie Biggs actually did very well out of the kidnapping. Not only did he retain his freedom but it put him firmly back on the media map as the number one celebrity criminal. Another book was written about his exploits and he co-wrote a feature film in 1984 called *Prisoner in Rio*, which flopped at the box office.

If it had not been for the kidnapping, his son Michael would not have been spotted by a Brazilian television producer who then made him the lead singer of a kiddies' pop group called Magic Balloon. With Michael an instant pop star, Biggs made a lot of money. It should have been the family's nest egg, giving them financial security for the rest of their lives but within a few short years it was all gone. As Michael today freely admits: 'My father and I blew it all on cocaine and stupidity.'

As for some of the other characters in Ronnie's life: Charmian Biggs still lives in Australia, while Raimunda became an 'exotic dancer' and lives in Switzerland. In Brazil, John and Lea Pickston remained Ronnie's closest friends looking after young Michael whenever necessary. Armin Heim however, Ronnie's self appointed bodyguard, was murdered in

Rio for being a paedophile. He was found with an axe imbedded in his skull.

By 2001, Ronnie's health had deteriorated considerably due to a series of strokes. With no money and now in need of constant medical assistance the fugitive could see no long-term future in Brazil. It was time to return to Britain and the good old welfare state. A deal was hatched between the media and Michael Biggs, so he could make some money, and his frail father was flown back to Britain and a waiting cell, with intermittent stays in the prison hospital. The family expected the British authorities to pardon Biggs immediately on his return but it was not to be. The fugitive would have to serve his sentence, or at least part of it, until parole was granted.

Ironically John Miller, the man who had originally thought up the idea of capturing Biggs, did not fulfil his ambition. He had hoped the Biggs affair would propel him into the movies. Instead the British Press became hostile to his antics and he moved to Los Angeles where he took a job as manager of a Country and Western club. But Hollywood and true stardom remained elusive. Undeterred, John decided to kick-start his career with another outrageous stunt. He approached ITN, the British television news agency, with an incredible story that he had found the fugitive Lord Lucan hiding on an island off the Florida coast. If it was true then ITN would have the scoop of a lifetime. John played on the fact that he had previously kidnapped Biggs and ITN would not risk passing up the chance of his Lucan story. They paid Miller between four and five thousand pounds, though nobody will admit the true amount, to take their reporter John Suchet and a crew to film the fugitive British peer. But the 'Lucan' they found was in fact one of Miller's associates, complete with false moustache. John took the money but the story had done him irreparable harm within the media.

Mark Algate, the former commando who had grabbed Ronnie in the Roda Vida restaurant, returned to Britain after the operation and eventually became a farmer.

Thorfinn Maciver the captain of the *Nowcani II* remained in the Caribbean where he continued to skipper luxury yachts for millionaire owners.

As for Tony Marriage, Fred Prime and myself, we stayed in the security business. In the avalanche of publicity that followed the Biggs kidnapping, our company, Point International Security – we often used the advertising slogan 'Assignments Unlimited' – was inundated with proposals, the more entertaining and bizarre of which could fill another book. We were asked to rescue children from religious sects, find buried gold in Uganda, repossess expensive yachts from Spain, buy seventy-six sofas in Rome for a Saudi Prince, organise African coups and dig up the family jewels buried in the cellar of a Russian *dacha*. One offer in particular tickled us: an Egyptian publisher in London asked us to distribute a magazine critical of a Middle Eastern regime, while, a few days later, a diplomat from that same regime hired us to find out who was distributing it!

The first serious pay-off from Ray Jarrett was a contract with the government of Uganda. President Milton Obote wanted to establish an intelligence-gathering unit under his direct control and based on the Rhodesian *Selous Scouts*, the finest special forces unit in Africa. Joining our team for this specialist job was Mike Borlace, a pilot and former member of the Selous Scouts. Our next Jarrett assignment was for Nigerian Governor Jim Nwobodo of Anambra State (formerly Biafra) who asked for experts to improve his State's security as well as provide protection for his stays in Britain.

By the mid-eighties Tony Marriage realised his thirst for adventure had been satisfied when he fell for the charms of a beautiful woman. He married Anne, had four children and became a paramedic serving the people of London.

Fred continued to work in security, enjoying protection assignments the most. He remained popular with his clients whether in show business or industry. Even Ronnie Biggs had a soft spot for his 'babysitter'.

Later, I decided to expand my media interests and began to carve a career in television. I became one of the producers on the highly rated *The Cook Report* featuring investigative journalist Roger Cook. Since then I have made many documentary films and won several awards. But Ronnie Biggs was to be part of my life yet again when, in 2005, I was asked to tell the real story of his abduction from Brazil.

IN SEARCH OF JARRETT

I first met Sylvia Jones when we were both working for Central Television's *The Cook Report* and soon became good friends. Before becoming a television producer, Sylvia had been chief crime correspondent of the *Daily Mirror* and was known in the media as a person with excellent contacts both in the police and other more secretive government agencies. She was one of the very few people who knew about my involvement in the Ronald Biggs affair and realised there was more to the kidnap than had ever been made public.

John Miller and Biggs were the only people who had ever talked about the affair and their versions kept changing with the years. Fred Prime, Tony Marriage and I, on the other hand, had never talked publicly. A deal was struck with British broadcasters Channel 4 and I became a co-producer on *Kidnap Ronnie Biggs.*

From the outset I made it clear to the other producers that I believed it was the British Establishment who were the secret backers of the kidnap plot. But how to prove it?

There was some evidence in my own rapid rise in the field of international security work within six months of the Biggs affair. There was the proof of contracts I had fulfilled with foreign governments as well as other high-profile clients. I brokered assignments for Sir David Stirling, founder of the SAS, including the organising of a training school in Oklahoma run by British and American special forces personnel and I had a letter from Margaret Thatcher wishing my company luck in the venture. I had attended numerous functions where Mrs Thatcher was present and would not have been allowed within ten feet of the Prime Minister if I had not been vetted.

But was it really a British government agency behind the kidnap? As far as we were concerned, the only man who could say for sure was Ray Jarrett – but how to find him? With no guarantee that he had even used his real name, there was little to go on. To assist Sylvia Jones, a researcher named James Oliver was hired and the search for Jarrett began.

Jarrett was possibly over eighty by now and many of the people involved in 1981 had either retired or died. For instance, attempts to find Major Halford, who first introduced me to Jarrett, failed. All the Major Halford's who fitted the profile in terms of age and regiment were dead.

Our best lead was the New York telephone number I had written down for Jarrett all those years ago. By running checks on the number we obtained an address. Old commercial directories revealed the number was located at 25 Central Park West. I was stunned, I knew the address. I had done business there, not in 1981 but later in 1984 with an American businessman called Wake Warthen.

In 1981, the number was registered to a firm of attorneys called Robb & Reukauf. It was possible that Ray Jarrett hired a room in the attorney's offices while in New York. Then came another revelation! By cross-referencing various sources, we established that one of the eponymous attorneys was Scott Robb. Further research revealed that in 1984 Scott Robb went into the communications business with a company called Worldcom Radio Services. His partner was a man named Wake Warthen. Bingo! There was our link.

I first met Wake Warthen in Nigeria when we were working for Chief Jim Nwobodo, Governor of Anambra State. Both Wake and I got our respective contracts from a young Nigerian businessman called Emeka Onah. Onah was introduced to me by Ugandan businessman Fred Bananuka. It was Bananuka who had brokered my deal with the Ugandan Government, and he was introduced to me by Ray Jarrett. A coincidence? Well there are not many coincidences in this business! The paper trail was beginning to take shape.

The second link with the address was an American named Al Boyles, a former CIA agent, who knew Jarrett and Wake Warthen. In 1986 Boyles arranged for my company to give a series of high-level security seminars in New York and Dallas. My main speakers included Pete Flynn, the SAS aviation expert, Colonel Tim Spicer, later to become one of the biggest names in private security, and Andrew Thompson who was Prime Minister Margaret Thatcher's personal political agent. It was high-powered stuff in front of some leading US companies including American Airlines and American Express. Wake Warthen also attended.

Sylvia Jones was intrigued by all this but she needed to talk to someone other than myself who had met Jarrett. Al Boyles was dead. Scott Robb and Wake Warthen remained silent, so that left only Fred Bananuka in Uganda. When Sylvia finally tracked down Fred in Kampala he was very cooperative and spoke in detail about Jarrett. He explained how Jarrett had put my name forward to the government when he visited Uganda.

In the meantime, other details about the Biggs kidnap were trickling through. Jim Sewell, commander of Scotland Yard's Flying Squad in 1981, told Sylvia that he attended a meeting with his boss, Metropolitan Police Commissioner David MacNee, who stated that bringing Biggs back would prove to be too much hassle. I find it hard to believe that Scotland Yard wouldn't want Britain's most wanted fugitive back in gaol, unless they were told this was not a politically viable solution.

The government was getting fearful that long-standing trade deals between Britain and Brazil were now in jeopardy of collapsing. Respected BBC producer Mike Duttfield, who had investigated the Biggs affair back in 1981, told me that he believed the trade deal was worth over £150 million, half a billion pounds at today's values. The stakes were certainly high and you can just imagine the agitation in the Foreign Office as they searched for the official who had instigated this new Biggs crisis. We decided to ask the Foreign Office to comment and to see if we could speak to someone who was on the Brazil desk at the time. The Foreign Office declined to help – even after twenty-five years.

As part of my commitment to Channel 4, I was required to re-visit the locations of the operation. It was certainly strange to return to Brazil, now a democracy with a thriving economy. I do like the Brazilians and their zest for life, however, fifty per cent of the population live below the poverty line and violence is still part of everyday life. In 1981 the murder rate in Rio was 2,800 a year, twenty-five years later it is 8,500 a year. We talked to several Brazilians, including policemen, all of whom believed the kidnap was orchestrated by the British Establishment.

My belief is the operation was financed from a military intelligence 'slush fund'. Sylvia also thought that was possible and contacted a retired British General who had been in military intelligence in the 1980s. Although personally unaware of any such assignment, he did agree that our theory was conceivable; bizarrely, he thought the budget for the operation rather small! At the end of our long research several interesting facts had emerged to support my story.

We now knew that in the 1980s, the one area where Britain felt most frustrated in its battle with terrorism was in its inability to bring known terrorists to justice. Extradition, or the lack of it, was the single most contentious issue in Anglo-Irish relations due to the Irish Courts' repeated refusal to hand over IRA suspects for trial in Britain. Similar problems applied to IRA men in the USA where politicians and judges were prone to exempt suspects from extradition to the UK on the grounds that their activities were political.

We also knew that Military Intelligence had expanded their

activities outside the British Isles against the IRA. We learnt that British Intelligence had been operating front companies in major American cities to gather information on IRA suspects as well as Irish American fund raisers. Jarrett had said he was working for an American client and I did meet him twice at the Algonquin Hotel in Manhattan. Sylvia contacted a retired senior FBI agent who knew about British activities during that period. Based on his own experience he thought our story was very probable indeed. He also reminded us that Central and South America, with its abundance of 'banana republics', has always been a haven for terrorists and criminals from all over the world. So was it possible that the Biggs operation was set up to test the extradition process from that region?

Extradition treaties invariably contain a loophole – the 'political offence exception' – which has frequently frustrated the United States in its efforts to extradite foreign terrorists who profess their crimes to be political in nature. The exception has often been applied by politically sympathetic courts, ironically by the Americans themselves when expedient, who have hindered the extradition from the United States of IRA terrorists.

The principle of political abduction goes back a long way. A notorious historical example was John Surratt, who was accused of complicity in the assassination of Abraham Lincoln, being snatched by US agents from Alexandria, Egypt, in 1866. Nearly a hundred years later Israeli agents kidnapped Nazi war criminal Adolf Eichmann from Argentina. Eichmann was seized, bundled onto a plane chartered by the Israeli government and flown to Israel. Argentina vehemently protested the kidnap as a violation of its sovereignty.

Since the Biggs affair in 1981 these methods have been increasingly employed. In 1990, the FBI sent agents to Cuba to kidnap rogue financier Robert Vesco, the plan being to take him to the Dominican Republic from where he could be extradited. It had all the hallmarks of the Biggs operation. In

1992, Dr Humberto Alvarez-Machain, a Mexican physician, was abducted from his office in Guadalajara, Mexico, and flown in a private plane to El Paso, Texas. It is widely accepted that the kidnap of former Yugoslav President Slobodan Milosevic was organised by MI6 (the British Secret Intelligence Service) before he was taken to the International Criminal Tribunal in the Hague. With the advent of the 'War on Terror', state kidnapping has become a matter of policy, with victims being taken from Afghanistan and elsewhere without legal process before being held in prisons around the world – most notably Guantanamo Bay in Cuba – without trial.

My opinion is the same as in 1981 – kidnapping Ronnie was an obsession of the British Establishment. It was a deniable action sanctioned by people with influence and money. Some cynics have suggested it was a stunt to earn money from media sales. But the cost of the operation was $100,000 – worth nearly half a million today – too big an investment to recoup from the media, in those days anyway. I believe that the most ever paid by a national newspaper at that time to an individual for a story was $60,000 for Britt Ekland's bedroom exploits!

Did the Establishment, Scotland Yard, the Spooks, or whoever, get value for money? Only they can answer that. But at least it was a stunt that fascinated the public and, importantly, nobody got hurt.

When all is said and done – it was one hell of a caper!